praise for

The Change Your Life Challenge

Over ninety thousand women have used Brook Noel's *Change Your Life Challenge* (*CYLC*) self-improvement tools since 2005.

"*CYLC* is a powerful tool for making very effective changes toward a greater quality of life. It has guided, inspired, and motivated me to cultivate better relationships with those I love, create a more peaceful home, adopt a joyful outlook, and connect with my authentic self. I recommend it highly to anyone wanting to take deliberate steps toward a fuller, more rewarding life." —Sarah, Pennsylvania

"This book has changed my life already and I've only been following it for a week! I know that may sound dramatic, but along with the support from others via the message board, I can already feel the benefits. A very interesting plan. Extremely well-written. A must-have for any busy woman." —Kathleen, UK

"I just started this program and it has already changed my life. The Catch-All notebook is indeed my new best friend. My mind is so uncluttered now. If this is the impact the first week has had on my life, I can't wait to see how it looks at the end! God bless you for developing this program!" —Brittany, California

"I am halfway through this program and have seen DRAMATIC changes to my life already. This challenge has really helped me to FOCUS on what is important in my life and to achieve it in tiny steps. I am glad to be a challenge participant and am telling everyone I know to take this challenge. I can already feel it making changes in my life." — Lana, West Texas

"I've used planners, Lotus Organizer (my life! I love it — syncs with my PDA), MS Project, but nothing actually kept me on track the way the *CYLC* Catch-All Notebook and the Action Item List has." — Pat, Indiana

"Self-help books have been around for a long time, but sadly readers usually don't change much after reading them. But Brook Noel has provided an easy-to-follow guide to make some long-lasting changes to bring organization and direction to your life. Don't procrastinate any longer in changing your life into the one you know you are meant to enjoy." — Diane, Arizona

"The *CYLC* has taught me that life is much more pleasant when it isn't a race or out of control. I have realized that anyone can be well-rounded and have everything that matters when they have continuous support, goals, and a course of action for life. By using this system, I no longer feel like I just exist, but that I am actually living and getting to where I want to be." — Lynda, Ontario

"My life has felt like chaos for several months (years?) and reading about the *CYLC* came at a critical time in my life. I am on Step 10 and get so excited to read each new Step. I am getting more done in the past few days than I was accomplishing in the past few months. I was feeling paralyzed by the volume of things I had to do, and now feel like I can move freely through my day! Thank you so much for creating this challenge!" — Lisa, New Mexico

"This is a program that showed me there is an easier way to manage my house and children than going crazy every day hunting things down. The system really works and, with little time given up to get things rolling, I have family time back again and that is truly a gift. Thanks Brook Noel!" —Dorothy, England

"I am glad I decided to take this *Change Your Life Challenge* because it's one of the best things I have done for myself in a long time. I think everyone should get this book and try it because it can change your life for the better. I now like the words 'clean house'!" —Lizzy, Minnesota

"I was skeptical about another book on change. I never have enough time and am constantly looking for keys, kids' homework, lists I made, etc. I have been working through this for a month and I can already see differences and find that I actually spend a lot less time looking for things with my favorite new item as the Catch-All Notebook. I highly recommend Noel's book. I felt like she could really understand my needs as a busy parent, wife and friend." —Steph, Dallas

"I've made soooooooooo much progress that my hubby is getting me a dishwasher this weekend. I've never had one." —Beth, California

"Starting the day with a Good Morning and doing a nightly reflection and ending with Gratitude started to make fundamental changes in my life paradigm that make me a better woman, mother and wife, I don't feel so stressed out, racing and putting out fires. I do a lot more preventative maintenance." —Lori, Maine

"I have seen changes in my life because of this challenge. I just wanted to let you know that your words of wisdom are helping one gal from Texas keep it all together." —Deena, Texas

"Finally, a simple plan to follow. This is helping me and changing me for the better. I am so grateful to have found this book, and to apply it in my life. When days get busy, I stick around on a certain day, and it only enforces the habit! This is a really great book: stick with it one day at a time, and you too will see changes for the better!" — Heather, Illinois

"This book is geared toward the busy person in search of ways to get more organization in their life and it truly works! The plan helps you develop a routine for almost everything you need to do in your life to make it run smoothly. I am excited about the progress I am making towards organizing my life and making a better home for my family. For me, staying on task can be difficult, but with this program I also get the benefit of an online support group to help me stay focused and get back on task when I stray. Hats off to Brook Noel for creating a simple-to-follow plan of action that even I can manage." — Joan, Michigan

"Clear some space out of your schedule and work through Brook's system of getting organized, healthy, and financially responsible. Brook takes all the things in our lives that keep us off balance — from overstuffed closets to forgetting to take care of ourselves — and gives simple steps to create a balanced, simplified life. She also gives us a simple organizational system for managing our time, meal-planning ideas and things to make your relationships closer. If you are serious about making changes for the better, then this book is for you." — Elizabeth Dargis, "Simplicity Coach," Michigan

the
change your life
challenge

the
change your life
challenge

STEP-BY-STEP SOLUTIONS FOR
- **Finding Balance,**
- **Creating Contentment,**
- **Getting Organized, and**
- **Building the Life You Want**

BASED ON THE MAKE TODAY MATTER LIFE SYSTEM

Brook Noel

SOURCEBOOKS, INC.®
NAPERVILLE, ILLINOIS

Copyright © 2008 by Brook Noel
Cover and internal design © 2008 by Sourcebooks, Inc.
Cover photo © iStockphoto.com/Silberkorn

Published by Sourcebooks, Inc.
P.O. Box 4410, Naperville, Illinois 60567–4410
(630) 961–3900
Fax: (630) 961–2168
www.sourcebooks.com

Originally published in 2005 by Champion Press Ltd.

Library of Congress Cataloging-in-Publication Data

Noel, Brook.
  The change your life challenge : step-by-step solutions for finding balance, creating contentment, getting organized, and building the life you want / Brook Noel.
      p. cm.
  1. Women—Conduct of life. 2. Women—Life skills guides. 3. Success. I. Title.
BJ1610.N64 2008
646.7—dc22

                              2008009138

            Printed and bound in the United States of America.
                BG 10 9 8 7 6 5 4 3 2 1

I would like to dedicate this book to the many women who have joined me in the journey to make today matter.

Of special note are four women who have made the evolution of this program possible. Each of these women reached out and asked, "How can I give back to this program because this program has given me so much?" Rose Fields, Rhonda Miga, DeAnn Pierson, Lyn Witter — thank you for believing in this vision and for making it what it is today.

You make a difference and I am forever thankful and blessed by the fact your path crossed mine.

"Be the change you want to see in the world."—*Gandhi*

contents

introduction

Are You Ready for a Change?

"There are three types of people in this world: those who make things happen, those who watch things happen and those who wonder what happened. We all have a choice. You can decide which type of person you want to be. I have always chosen to be in the first group." —*Mary Kay Ash*

before we begin...

"Look at your past. Your past has determined where you are at this moment. What you do today will determine where you are tomorrow."— *Tom Hopkins*

I believe that you and I have a similar goal. I doubt you desire another book with ideas that do not work, which ultimately ends up dusty and requiring storage on an already-packed bookshelf. I do not want any dust on my book.

You want to change your life, or some part of it. Since 2005, this program has helped thousands of women, and it can help you too. But one solution will not work for everyone. I have paid close attention to the many success stories and what these women have in common.

You have likely read books in which the author spends paragraph upon paragraph advising you to put down the book and actually do an exercise or write something down. Yet many of us keep reading anyway. The author then puts big black letters or a stop sign to try and jar us from our habitual, inactive reading. We keep reading anyway. After all, we can always go back to the exercise, right? Certainly the book isn't going to walk away. Besides, maybe it makes more sense to read the whole thing through first— and then go back and do the activities. Right?

Or how about this: when was the last time you enrolled in an interactive program (school included) and completely disregarded instructions, avoided homework, and never took notes?

Simply put: you cannot apply these materials to your life successfully without doing the work. The women who succeed are active participants and apply the Steps thoroughly.

This program is not called the Think Your Life Challenge. You cannot do this all in your head. Success requires implementation, participation, and observation of personal patterns, goals, and desires. If you want to stop the tireless search for a solution and are ready to start living the solution, please proceed to page 3 and let's get started. The future awaits you!

how *the change your life challenge* can help you

"If you do not change directions, you may end up where you are heading."—*Lao-tzu*

If you are reading these words, then you are ready to change part (or many parts) of your life. Perhaps you are dissatisfied with your health or weight. Maybe you are exhausted and worn-out, feeling overwhelmed by life's seemingly continuous treadmill. Perhaps relationships with others are unfulfilling, negative, or toxic—or maybe you do not have enough relationships in your life. Maybe you have been on the never-ending hunt for "something more." Perhaps worry, anxiety, guilt, perfectionism, procrastination, or household management have become "too much." Whatever the area, you feel incomplete, but fortunately for us both, you are not willing to give up. You have likely tried multiple programs, organizational systems, and self-help tools. Instead of seeing success you likely saw money spent on a product that did not work longer than a month or two.

As the saying goes, "It takes one to know one." I was the aforementioned woman in every example. I was exhausted, stressed, worried, and dissatisfied with my day-to-day life. At the end of each day, I felt fatigued and incomplete instead of satisfied and happy. The magic of life had been replaced by stress, routine, and overcommitment.

I purchased every system I could find to try and implement self-change. After a decade of building a self-help library that could compete with the Library of Congress, I paused and reflected on each of the books I had read, tapes I had heard, and theories I had tried. I evaluated each program by asking: *Why didn't this work for me?* I quickly uncovered a pattern.

1. **I tried to make a very big change at a time when my resources were depleted.**

    Often, when we attempt to change, we are not feeling that great about ourselves or our lives. Who starts a diet or eating plan when they are pleased with their body? We are more likely to begin after trying to squeeze into pants that once fit and now cannot be pulled past our knees. In this disenchanted state, we try to revamp food and exercise overnight. Then we become frustrated when we cannot continue with rigorous (often unrealistic) expectations for more than several weeks (if that).

2. **Programs rarely focus on multi-dimensional change.**

    Many programs focus on changing only actions or thoughts. We do not become dissatisfied through just actions or just thoughts, however, but through a combination of ineffective actions and non-directed or negative thoughts. To create any lasting change, we cannot focus exclusively on changing our thinking and assume our actions will change. Likewise, we cannot focus exclusively on changing our actions to transform our thoughts. While these types of programs will produce short-term results, lasting change requires a dual effort, working back and forth between thought and action.

3. **Many programs are too complicated!**

    Just because our lives are complicated, our solutions do not need to be! Much of our dissatisfaction is derived from lack of time. We don't have time to eat right, exercise, communicate with all of our friends, family, and children, do household maintenance, and _____ (add your own 1001 item to-do list). A complicated system only compounds internal confusion and frustration.

4. **The action steps require a week's vacation.**

I have attended many workshops and read many books full of wonderful ideas. Unfortunately, each step would require a week off from work and family for proper implementation. Even when I could accomplish one step, undoubtedly life's pressures would bear down during the second step and I would abandon the program. We are all working with 24/7 schedules, and any practical, attainable program must recognize this, and fit within the many commitments we already have. Drastic and short-term change can be built on drastic steps, but lasting change is built by strategic, attainable small steps.

5. **There was a missing link.**

I agreed wholeheartedly with the wisdom contained in many programs; however, I had no idea how to implement this wisdom into my day-to-day life. Without a breakdown of practical action steps, I was left with great ideas but no plan.

6. **When I became stuck, resources were not available to answer my questions or help me overcome a hurdle.**

Whenever we try something new, we will face hurdles. When I faced these hurdles, rarely was there an efficient way to get help or ask questions. When help existed it often required traveling to a specific "support group" on a certain day at a certain time. While some programs offered Internet support, they were not moderated at a level that allowed me to feel safe within the community. Without an efficient way to move forward, I stopped.

7. **The program did not take into account my individual needs and action style.**

Many programs proceed at a set pace and in a set order. This one-size-fits-all solution focuses on what the program needs to be, versus what I need from the program. If I do not match the program, eventually it becomes impossible to maintain.

Why Self-Improvement Programs Often Fail after a Week

"If I could just get _____ under control, everything would be fine..." Feeling out of balance, a person seeks a solution for the life area where imbalance is perceived, in turn moving away from the "core" self.

When I completed my analysis of over twelve hundred books, products, planners, and programs, I decided to take these observations and devote my life to creating programs tailored to overcome these seven major stopping points.

THE SELF-IMPROVEMENT CYCLE GONE BAD (REAL BAD)

When faced with a challenge, a woman often purchases a solution geared toward the area she hopes to change. In doing so, she actually moves away from her core self by reaching outward. This "moving away" explains how the more a woman tries to change, the less satisfaction she finds. She is looking for satisfaction externally, and external satisfaction fluctuates like the weather and is not long-lived. No wonder women often feel pulled in a million directions: as shown in the illustration on page 6, indeed we are!

Remember the concept of "spot-toning" in fitness? Focusing on a set of exercises to flatten the stomach or slim the thighs? Spot-toning was created by a society interested in fast fixes. If we focus exclusively on our abs, and neglect the other areas, we may find the desired sculpted tummy, but surely other areas will lose tone. Most self-improvement programs are the equivalent of spot-toning for life. A Band Aid is applied to one area while the other areas become neglected or infected.

THE CHALLENGE, NEW AND IMPROVED

This is actually the second iteration of the *Change Your Life Challenge*. Prior to the first edition of this book, I spent eighteen months testing my program online. Over three thousand people took the *Change Your Life Challenge*. Since the first edition, over ninety thousand women have heard about The Challenge and taken part in its various programs. The biggest satisfaction I ever had was the discovery of how this program helped the many women who were convinced they had "tried everything," and that "nothing else could possibly work."

In the three years I have worked with the initial program, I have gathered feedback from over ten thousand women. I am pleased that its success has allowed the creation of this new edition which provides even more tools, ideas, and action steps based on the feedback of program participants.

This brand-new, fully revised edition provides an integrated, balanced approach for creating the life you desire. The journey you are about to embark on provides a proven way to determine your core needs and priorities and create a lifestyle of ongoing balance and contentment tailored to you.

The Change Your Life Challenge book is a do-it-yourself, portable life-makeover. Its Toolbox is packed with 15 Steps from the Make Today Matter Life System to help you take control, regain balance, recover energy, and approach change in a new way – a way that sticks. The Mini-Makeovers provide a springboard for ongoing improvement based on the tailored action plan in the program. At any time you can return to the book, create a new action plan, and quickly find proactive strategies to implement.

The Make Today Matter Life System Online (MTM) is my second program, which I founded in 2008 in response to the overwhelming reception of **The Change Your Life Challenge***.*

MTM is comprised of a 30-Step Toolbox, ongoing Mini-Makeovers, and a complete community and support network for implementing the program. Each month I walk members through the process of creating an action plan online. Within this supportive framework, members then choose which Mini-Makeovers to apply based on the needs revealed by their action plans.

HOW TO MAKE *THE CHANGE YOUR LIFE CHALLENGE* WORK FOR YOU!

Prior to creating the *Challenge*, whenever I purchased a program one of the first things I wanted to know was — *how long until it is over?* I was usually in a place in which I needed change yesterday and the thought of going slowly drove me nuts. I am an overachiever, "Type A" personality who wants it all — *and wants it all now!* The *Change Your Life Challenge* is carefully designed to ensure maximum success for each participant. For that reason, it is important to follow the instructions as written — even if, like me, *you want it all now*.

This book is divided into three parts:

1. Five Steps to a Successful Start
2. The Toolbox
3. Mini-Makeovers

Five Steps to a Successful Start: I will walk you step-by-step through building a solid foundation for the journey ahead. First, we will complete your first Snapshot: an inventory of where you are and where you want to be in sixteen Life Areas. I'll also share additional free online resources, walk you through the creation of an Action Plan, and introduce the basic supplies and how to set them up for success. Complete this section at whatever pace you desire.

The Toolbox: After completing the Snapshot, you can dive into the Toolbox. Within this Toolbox are fifteen Steps that create positive change when applied to *any* Life Area. These Steps are not optional; they are the bricks that build a solid foundation for your *Challenge*. No matter what findings your Snapshot reveals, these tools will help you live a life of balance and contentment, recover energy, build a positive outlook, manage time, and take effective action.

You have to actually do the Steps — reading through them and thinking about them will not yield change. I only bring this up because I have also tried that strategy in the past. Once you have one Step down, move on to the next. The only caveat: do not implement more than one Step per day. Two days per week (you can pick which two), continue working with what you have learned to date, but do not add a new Step. **I understand some of you *really* want to skip that last sentence and you are the people who need to re-read it.** Moving any faster creates a high likelihood that you will burn out at some point. Science has shown that our mind needs time to assimilate, understand, and apply new information. Successful program participants read and implement only one Step per day and take two days off each week. You might think you can do it differently — and technically you can. But one word of warning: this program is a "perfect" recipe. Changing it is like substituting an ingredient in a recipe—who knows what you will cook up.

Mini-Makeovers: The Mini-Makeover Collection provides five-step makeovers for key Snapshot Areas. Another Snapshot is completed before beginning this section, since many of your numbers may change from applying the Steps you learn in the Toolbox. This second Snapshot will determine the order for working through the Mini-Makeover section.

AND NOW...

It is time to begin. When you are ready, continue to the Five Steps to a Successful Start to begin the journey.

PART ONE

five steps to a successful start

"Luck is a crossroad where preparation and opportunity meet."
—*Anonymous*

This section contains five steps to prepare for the *Change Your Life Challenge*. Work through these Steps at whatever pace you like, and then proceed to Part Two: The Toolbox.

Getting Started Step 1:   **Setting Up Shop**

Getting Started Step 2:   **The Snapshot**

Getting Started Step 3:   **Creating Your Action Plan for Change**

Getting Started Step 4:   **The Headquarters Binder**

Getting Started Step 5:   **Rally Your Resources**

getting started step 1

Setting Up Shop

"Don't let the fear of the time it will take to accomplish something stand in the way of your doing it. The time will pass anyway; we might just as well put that passing time to the best possible use."—*Earl Nightingale, speaker, author*

All long-term successes are built on solid foundations. Most of the time, when we implement a change, we want the change to occur *now*. In our eagerness to realize change, we often skip the process of building a solid foundation. We begin with a "go-get-'em" attitude, only to crumble a few days or weeks later when our foundation is faulty.

Since you didn't get into an organizational upheaval overnight, keep in mind that it takes baby steps to get out. The premise of this program is that simple efforts, made consistently, will yield significant results over time.

Before leaving for any important trip, we need to pack carefully. Packing for the *Change Your Life Challenge* journey requires a few inexpensive common supplies. (Make sure to check around your home first!)

CHANGE YOUR LIFE CHALLENGE SUPPLY LIST
- One three-ring binder, one-inch capacity
- One set of eight blank tabs that will fit into a three-ring binder
- Loose-leaf, lined paper

- A small spiral notebook that can lay flat, such as a four-by-six- or five-by-seven-inch, eighty- to one-hundred-page notebook. (This notebook will need to go with you everywhere as you will learn in Step One of the Toolbox. If you carry a purse or bag, choose a size that fits easily within.)
- A notebook for recording thoughts and reflections. (Throughout the Challenge, this will be referred to as your journal. A regular letter-size one-subject spiral notebook works best. Avoid fancy journals as they can be intimidating to write in and we have a lot to put in here!)
- One hundred three-by-five-inch white index cards (lined on one-side, blank on the other) or printable index card templates. (Consider Avery #5388, which are compatible with free online resources.)
- Five to ten nine-by-twelve-inch paper envelopes (any color)
- Yellow highlighter
- Four self-adhesive clear pouches or self-adhesive photo-pockets that can hold a three-by-five inch index card
- Hole punch
- Scissors
- Stapler
- Tape
- Two durable plastic expanding envelopes with a one-inch capacity, with inside dimensions capable of holding several magazines

OPTIONAL:
The items below are not required but come in handy for easy organizing.
- Several folders or pockets to insert on the rings of your three-ring binder
- Plastic sheet/page protectors
- Three-hole paper punch
- Printing paper that is three-hole drilled (for printing worksheets without manual punching)

Several of the Mini-Makeovers have a few additional supply suggestions. It is best to wait until you move to the Mini-Makeovers to add these extra supplies.

TAKE A STEP FORWARD

Check your home for any supplies you may already have on hand and then make a trip to purchase the rest. You will need to have these supplies for Step 4.

Visit www.brooknoelstudio.com for links to online suppliers and our Change Your Life Challenge product line.

getting started step 2

The Snapshot

"I am looking forward to looking back on all of this." —*Sandra Knell*

Albert Einstein stated, "The definition of insanity is doing the same thing over and over and expecting different results." We don't want to make the same mistake we have in the past and jump into "yet another solution" because we are unhappy with some aspect of our life. When we jump, we set ourselves up for failure in two ways:

1. We do not stop and truly assess what we want to change.
2. We don't look at our life in its entirety to see what needs to be changed.

Oftentimes we buy a book, program, workbook, or audiotape because the topic or "promise" strikes a chord. On a whim, we make the purchase, hoping it will help us create change. Usually it doesn't. When we approach change without clearly assessing our needs, then our needs will be impossible to fulfill. We cannot find a solution without first identifying what needs solving.

Today we will be taking a Snapshot of your life. Don't cringe and close the book! I realize this isn't going to be a glorious snapshot—if it was, you wouldn't be taking the *Challenge*. That is okay. I was hardly satisfied when I invented this program. In fact, if it weren't for my dissatisfaction, this program would not exist. Think of this Snapshot as the "before picture"—it's not supposed to be pretty. Rest assured, the "after" isn't far away!

The Snapshot is a tool used throughout the program. Even after the completion of the *Challenge,* a monthly Snapshot allows a "quick view" of where we are, and what Life Areas we might focus on to increase balance and satisfaction.

SNAPSHOT BASICS AND PREPARATION

The Snapshot is comprised of categories representing Life Areas. Next to each category is a row of boxes numbered one through ten. These rows represent Personal Priority Scales. A ten represents high-priority areas during this season of your life, whereas a one represents areas that are not a priority right now. I use the term "seasons of life" because priorities often shift. Sometimes these shifts occur monthly, other times quarterly, other times annually or every couple of years. This Snapshot is not meant to capture your priorities for your entire life — only the current season and your priorities today, at this moment.

> *If you do not want to write in your book, before reading further make a photocopy or print an additional copy by visiting www.brooknoelstudio.com*

CUSTOMIZING THE SNAPSHOT

In the category list there are three categories that may or may not apply to you:

- **Relationship with children:** If you do not have children, this would not apply to you.
- **Relationship with partner:** If you are not in a relationship, this would not apply to you.
- **Main Hat:** The Main Hat category reflects the primary responsibility of your waking hours. Attending school, volunteering, working, homeschooling, or running the home are some examples. If you do not have a primary activity which consumes a large portion of your waking

Snapshot .... Taken on _____ (Date, Month, Year)

* To determine the Tally Number, subtract the Life Number from the Journey Number.

General Life Area	Description	10	9	8	7	6	5	4	3	2	1	Journey Number	Life Number	Tally*
Time Management	The general ability to mange time and effectively achieve obligations, commitments and goals	10	9	8	7	6	5	4	3	2	1	9	5	4
Information Management	Ability to manage information (so you can find a number or password as needed), paper management (including filing)	10	9	8	7	6	5	4	3	2	1	9	6	3
Relationships	Relationship with significant other	10	9	8	7	6	5	4	3	2	1			
	Relationship with children (whether grown or in the home)	10	9	8	7	6	5	4	3	2	1			
	Relationship with friends (such as a support network and positive friends you spend time with regularly)	10	9	8	7	6	5	4	3	2	1	6	7	-1
Money Management	Including debt, general financial health, savings goals, budgeting and smart-spending	10	9	8	7	6	5	4	3	2	1	10	2	8
Self Time	Time devoted exclusively to self-care, self-growth, rejuvenation	10	9	8	7	6	5	4	3	2	1	6	3	3
Attitude and Outlook	The ability to maintain a positive outlook and attitude	10	9	8	7	6	5	4	3	2	1	8	5	3
Self-Esteem	How you personally feel about yourself overall	10	9	8	7	6	5	4	3	2	1	6	4	2
Household Maintenance	Includes having your home organized how you want, decluttered to a level of your liking, and maintaining routine tasks	10	9	8	7	6	5	4	3	2	1	4	8	-4
Health	Including nutrition, food consumption and overall health	10	9	8	7	6	5	4	3	2	1	4	8	-4
Energy	Your general physical energy level	10	9	8	7	6	5	4	3	2	1	4	6	-2
Religion and spirituality	Religion, faith or spiritual practice	10	9	8	7	6	5	4	3	2	1	4	3	1
Community	Giving back to the community through volunteering or another connection	10	9	8	7	6	5	4	3	2	1			
Main Hat	The area you spend most of your time for example occupation, homeschooling, volunteering	10	9	8	7	6	5	4	3	2	1			5
Meal Planning	Routine meal planning and solutions	10	9	8	7	6	5	4	3	2	1		6	4

hours (perhaps you are retired and pursuing many different interests), then this category would not apply to you.

If any of these three categories do not apply to you, place an X through the category name. (Use a pencil on your first Snapshot.) Other categories may seem to be irrelevant at this point in your life, but do not cross them off. Only the three aforementioned categories can be deleted.

CREATING A COMPARISON POINT

What is the primary reason or motivator for you picking up this book? Out of the categories listed, what category best contains your prime motivator? Place a star next to the category title.

HOW TO COMPLETE THE SNAPSHOT

Completing the Snapshot involves three steps:

1. Defining your Journey Numbers
2. Uncovering your Life Numbers
3. Three Portraits: Journey, Life, and Action

It is best to complete all three steps in one sitting.

STEP 1: DEFINING YOUR JOURNEY NUMBERS

Begin by carefully considering the category in the first row: Time Management. How important is time management to you right now? If it is very important, circle one of the higher numbers. If it is not important to you right now, choose one of the lower numbers. If it is somewhere between high-importance and low-importance; choose one of the middle numbers. The circled number is your Journey Number. The only factor this number reflects is how important this area is to you *right now*. It does not reflect where you currently perceive yourself to be, where you think you should be, or where you are in comparison to your next-door neighbor.

As women, we often fall into the "please everyone—sacrifice ourselves" trap. We want to be everything to everyone and then ride the roller coaster of guilt when we cannot achieve this impossible standard. I know what that Snapshot looks like—I've tried it. I do not want to see that on your worksheet. Instead, I want you to try something that might be a bit foreign. Let your choices be reflective of what *you* truly want from *your* life, not what others want for you or what will make others happy.

When our life is out of balance, every Life Area may be clamoring for our attention. We may feel the urge to give every category an eight, nine, or ten. If you have this challenge, try comparing each category to the comparison point you starred in the first step, which is likely a nine or ten. For example if you starred "Nutrition," ask yourself: "How important is time management in comparison to nutrition?" Right now, is it equally important, less important, or somewhere in-between? Circle a number reflective of your answer. A lower number does not mean the area is not important or will be ignored. A lower number only indicates that other life areas are higher on your life radar at the moment.

Keep in mind that no one will see this Snapshot. It is just for you. The only "right answer" is honesty. Our Snapshot is as unique as our thumbprint. Maybe your high-importance areas would seem odd to another person. We aren't creating this Snapshot for another person. We are creating this Snapshot to help you identify and create a path to fulfill the unique needs that brought you here.

Work through each category of the Snapshot in the same way.

Please complete this step before continuing.

STEP 2: YOU ARE HERE! UNCOVERING YOUR LIFE
NUMBERS

The completed area of the Snapshot indicates how you would like
your life to look. Your next step is to identify where you are *right
now* in relation to your Journey Numbers.

Look at your Journey Number in the Time Management category.
How would that number "look" in your life? What would change?
Take a moment to imagine how your life would be different at that
Journey Number.

Next consider how well you currently manage time. Which of
the following statements best describes the relationship between
your day-to-day reality and your Journey Number?

- My Journey Number and my current reality are the same.
- My current reality needs to change in order to reach my
  Journey Number.
- My current reality exceeds my Journey Number.

Now place a square around a number that reflects your answer.
For example:

- My Journey Number and my current reality are the same.
  Place a square around your Journey Number.
- My current reality needs to change in order to reach my
  Journey Number. Place a square around a number below
  your Journey Number. The larger the gap between your current reality and your ideal, the lower you would place the
  square.
- My current reality exceeds my ideal. Place a square around a
  number above your Journey Number. The more you exceed
  your ideal, the higher you would place the square.

The numbers marked with squares are called your "Life
Numbers." Work through each category and mark a Life Number.

Please complete this step before continuing.

STEP 3: SUMMARIZING YOUR FINDINGS—THREE PORTRAITS

We now have two types of information about your life:

- **Journey Profile:** The Journey Profile is comprised of all the circled Journey Numbers, and provides an overview of where you want to be.
- **Life Profile:** The Life Profile is comprised of all of the squared Life Numbers, and provides an overview of where you are today.

Our last step involves merging these two findings together to create an Action Snapshot.

The right-most column is labeled "tally." Subtract your squared number from the circled number and write the result in this box.

For example, if you circled a nine in finances for your Journey Number, and then placed a square around five for your Life Number, the total would be four (9–5=4). If your Journey Number was a six and your Life Number was an eight, the tally would be negative two (6–8=-2). These numbers, this Action Snapshot, form the foundation for the Action Plan we create in the next Chapter.

TAKE A STEP FORWARD

Complete the Snapshot by following the instructions in this Step.

getting started step 3

Creating Your Action Plan for Change

"Action is the antidote to despair." —*Joan Baez*

Educational systems have reasons they limit the number of majors students can take in a four-year-college program. Time, focus, and success rank high on the reason list. Imagine if one hundred students decided to declare five majors simultaneously. In four years, they aimed to complete marine biology, art history, mass communications, psychiatry, and primary education. Given the time and focus required by each major, what do you think the success rate of these one hundred students would be?

No matter what the students' willpower, intelligence, desire, optimism, stamina, or energy-level, this lofty goal cannot be reached. There are not enough hours in a day to complete five demanding majors in a four-year period.

In the end, all of these students would fail. Does this mean they are bad students? Of course not (although they may interpret incompletion as failure). The missing link is not in their attitude, energy, or ability to take action. The missing component is time.

Change requires focus, and focus requires time. In order to achieve change, we need to replace ingrained habits with new actions and choices. Trying to implement multiple lofty changes in addition to maintaining day-to-day responsibilities creates an environment nonconducive to focus. Without focus we cannot complete what we start.

Focus, not desire or willpower, is at the core of cycling through one program after another. Without a clearly defined plan for change containing concise action steps, we are swimming upstream. The *Change Your Life Challenge* program and is designed to encourage focus, which in turn increases the success rate of lasting lifestyle change.

COMPLETING THE ACTION PLAN FOR CHANGE WORKSHEET

It is time to create our Action Plan, using the information we have gathered. Find the Action Plan worksheet, take your tallies (Journey Number minus Life Number), and then follow these steps:

1. Zero:

    Look for any categories that equal zero. A zero means that your results and priority are in alignment. Write the names of these categories in the "Balanced: Manage & Maintain" box. (Don't worry if you do not have any zeroes—you will soon!)

2. Negative Numbers:

    Look for any negative numbers in your Action Snapshot tally column. (Don't worry if you don't have any negative numbers—few women do at the start.) A negative number means you are more than satisfied with your results in relation to the priority of that category in your life. If any of your negatively numbered categories involve a lot of time, consider scaling back your time to better align with the result you seek. Time gained can be used to focus on areas that are out of alignment. Write the names of any negative categories on the Action Plan worksheet in either the "Scale Back" box or "Balanced: Manage and Maintain" area.

3. Positive Numbers:

    Transfer the remaining categories, along with the tally number, to the Action Plan worksheet in the "Life Areas Needing Attention" box. List these numbers from high to low.

Action Plan Worksheet

Summary for Snapshot dated ___8/14/08___

Balance and Maintain

Relationships c Friends
Health
Energy
Spirituality
Meal Planning

Scale Back

Relationships w/ Mena

Life Area	Tally Number
List from high to low by tally number	
Money Management	8
Main Hat	5
Time Management	4
Information Man.	3
Self Time	3
Attitude and Outlook	3
Household maint	4
Self-Esteem	2
Community	1

Notes: _____

_____

_____

Quick Reference to Snapshot Categories:

Each category should be listed in one of the sections of the Action Plan worksheet.

Time Management	Religion and spirituality
Information Management	Community
Self-Time	Main Hat
Money Management	Meal Planning
Attitude and Outlook	Relationship with children
Relationship w/significant other	Relationship with friends
Health	Self-Esteem
Energy	Household Maintenance

Please complete this step before reading further.

READING THE RESULTS

We become stressed, overwhelmed, tired, and emotionally drained when our actions do not align with our values. Your Journey Profile offered a glimpse of how strongly you value each category at this phase of your life. Your Life Profile shows how closely your actions match your values. The Action Snapshot total provides a glimpse at which life areas have the largest gap between your actions and values; the higher the number, the greater the gap.

The list you created in the Action Plan worksheet is your personal checklist for working through the program. By filling the biggest gaps first, we recover energy, emotional well-being, and focus while creating forward momentum throughout the program.

After completing this worksheet, you may find the area you *want* to focus on is different than the area in most need of your attention. Avoid the temptation to work out of order. Don't try the entire exercise again to skew the results to match your wants. You have created a unique roadmap to take you from point A to point B. Follow your map. Keep the Action Plan worksheet handy to file in the Headquarters, the topic of the next Step.

TAKE A STEP FORWARD

Complete the Action Plan worksheet.

getting started step 4

The Headquarters

"You can have it all…just not at the same time." —*Unknown*

If you haven't yet purchased the supplies in Step 1: Setting Up Shop, take a quick trip to your local discount store or office supply store so you can set up the Headquarters in this Step.

Think of the Headquarters as the information desk of life. Just as you wouldn't transport a desk with you everywhere, the Headquarters should not be transported—it should have a permanent home. I recommend an area that is centrally located (so you have easy access to it) without being in a high-traffic zone. The last thing we want to happen is for your "beautiful base" to be rummaged through by a family member hunting down tape or scissors. Throughout the *Challenge,* you will be adding to this information desk.

Next, label the tab dividers from the supply list as follows:

1. SNAPSHOT

2. MONEY MATTERS

3. HOUSEWORK HELPERS

4. CONTACTS AND CONNECTIONS

5. HEALTH

6. PLANNING

7. FAMILY MATTERS

8. REFERENCE

Insert these tabs onto the rings of the three-ring binder. Place some white lined paper in the back of the binder. Hole-punch the Snapshot and Action Plan that you completed in Steps 2 and 3 and place behind the SNAPSHOT tab.

TAKE A STEP FORWARD

Complete the setup of your Headquarters.

getting started step 5

Rallying Your Resources

"Success becomes sustainable when there are environments and failsafe structures which support it and which make you feel fully alive. And being fully alive calls you to play a much bigger game in life...evolving to your optimal potential to levels of greatness you never thought were possible." —*Dave Buck*

The *Change Your Life Challenge* goes far beyond the book you hold in your hands. There are many resources available to you in addition to these pages. Understanding these support options, where to find them, and how to use them, will create a well-rounded support and resource system versus "just a book."

Sometimes a process, plan, or program seems like a "match" for life. A woman sets a start date and her excitement mounts. Then, life interrupts. She wakes up one day and decides to put the program off — for just a day. One day turns into another. She begins to believe that maybe this program was not the solution after all or maybe she just doesn't have what it takes. When goals are worked toward in isolation it is easy to build a list of reasons (or excuses) to turn back or abandon ship. Hope is replaced with letdown; excitement is replaced with frustration; opportunity is replaced with another dusty or unfinished book.

Encouragement, motivation, and support can be found in a group of positive women with similar goals, who can help overcome hurdles and answer questions when needed. When you are run-down or ready to give in, a group of like-minded women, in a similar place, at a similar time, facing similar challenges, can act as cheerleaders and accountability partners. I developed Make Today Matter as support for this journey.

THE MAKE TODAY MATTER LIFE SYSTEM ONLINE

The Make Today Matter Life System (MTM) provides an online supportive, moderated, positive community for women working to build contentment, balance, and a joy-filled life. In this ongoing program, the Toolbox Steps we'll cover in this book are reviewed, along with fifteen additional steps. Members complete a monthly Snapshot, creating a checklist of Life Areas to focus on.

The MTM program offers other benefits that cannot be offered in book form. While impossible to list them all, here is a highlight:

- **Toolbox Discussion:**
  Each Toolbox Step has a dedicated message board where you can ask questions, share experiences, and support one another.

- **Online Journal:**
  Optional reflection questions are offered in each member's private online journal.

- **Profile, Internal Messaging, and Online Chat:**
  Member's profiles and an internal mail system allow women easy ways to connect while keeping real email address and full names private.

- **Inspiration Library:**
  A library of articles, affirmation cards, quotes, and journal prompts.

- **Online Events:**
  The Action Jam Room provides moderated motivation seven days a week in a community chat room. Other online events include times to chat with me, special member-only work-shops, and cleaning marathon sprints.

- **Girls Night Out:**
  Designated "fun nights" for online game tournaments and camaraderie.

- **Rush Hour Meal Planning:**
  Printable weekly menus complete with shopping lists.

- **Resource Library:**
  The resource library is filled with printables, downloads, worksheets, and articles to support the Steps.

- **Motivation Moments:**
  Members can listen to my inspirational ideas online (or download them).

- **Quizzes and Rewards:**
  As members complete the Steps, Personal Power Cards are awarded (explained in Part Two, Step 6 of this book).

- **Mini-Makeovers:**
  Each month members can choose up to three new Mini-Makeovers to work on offline or within the community. You can browse the Mini-Makeover catalog at http://www.brooknoelstudio.com/

MAKE TODAY MATTER MINI-GROUPS (MTM GROUPS)
Many women benefit from forming a local group of women to connect and work with. Visit www.brooknoelstudio.com for guidelines and materials to start your own group or to locate an existing group.

USING THE *CHANGE YOUR LIFE CHALLENGE* BOOK INDEPENDENTLY

The *Change Your Life Challenge* provides a portable, independent guide for implementing my most popular self-improvement strategies on your own. You will find many free resource links and printable copies of the worksheets that appear within this book online at
http://www.brooknoelstudio.com/

Watch for this icon "☑" at the end of each Step to direct you to free resources.

STAYING IN THE LOOP

The Challenge Weekly is a free e-newsletter offering a personal challenge each week along with tools, tips, and ideas. Visit www.brooknoelstudio.com to begin your free subscription.

USING THE *CHANGE YOUR LIFE CHALLENGE* BOOK WITH MAKE TODAY MATTER SUPPORT

Combine the book with the online MTM program for ongoing improvement, motivation, and support.

If you are already a member, or join the MTM program, watch for the "☒" icon throughout this book for MTM resources to enhance your journey.

THE *CHANGE YOUR LIFE CHALLENGE* COMPANION WORKBOOK

The *Change Your Life Challenge Companion Workbook* contains blank worksheets and optional companion pages for the journey. These worksheets and journal pages measure eight-and-a-half-inches by eleven-inches for easy printing and plenty of writing room. This workbook is *only* available on CD or as an immediate digital download. This format allows for printing as many worksheets or planning sheets as needed. This workbook can be downloaded immediately at www.brooknoelstudio.com. (Please note this workbook is only available through the website.)

It is not necessary to purchase the workbook in order to complete the *Challenge;* we offer full-size versions of many of the forms you will see in this book free at http://www.brooknoelstudio.com. The workbook simply provides a one-stop solution and some form variations, tip sheets, and bonus material that would not all fit in the book.

> **Abbreviations:**
>
> **CYLC** is the abbreviation for the Change Your Life Challenge, the book.
>
> **MTM** is the abbreviation for the Make Today Matter Life System, the online community and materials on which this book is based.

TAKE A STEP FORWARD

Check off the actions you have completed below. Once all the boxes are checked you are ready to begin Part Two: The Toolbox.

- ☑ Read the program overview in the Are You Ready for a Change? Chapter.

- ☐ Compile the supplies listed in Step 1.

- ☑ Take your first Snapshot (Step 2).

- ☑ Follow the guidelines in Step 3 to create your Action Plan.

- ☐ Set up your Headquarters by following the instructions in Step 4. Add the Snapshot and Action Plan behind the SNAP-SHOT tab.

- ☑ Review the additional support resources detailed in Step 5.

- ☑ Decide if you will work through the program on your own, within a local group, or online in the MTM program.

- ☐ Visit and bookmark http://www.brooknoelstudio.com. Click on the free newsletter link to subscribe to *Challenge Weekly* newsletter if you like. Print a copy of the index of free resources, which lists all the free resources within the site. Tuck this in the book for handy reference. Alternatively, if you would like to purchase the Companion Workbook with all the printed worksheets in one file and bonus worksheets that would not fit in this book click the "shop" link from this page.

PART TWO

the toolbox

A Toolbox for Building Balance, Taking Action, Restoring Energy, and Transforming Chaos to Contentment

"I have found that if you love life, life will love you back." —*Arthur Rubenstein*

Step 1:   Meet the Catch-All Notebook (CAN)

Step 2:   The Three-Step Action List

Step 3:   How Do You Start Your Day?

Step 4:   The Catch-It Collectors

Step 5:   Moments of Magic

Step 6:   Soul Food: Creating a Personal Power Deck

Step 7:   The Five-Minute Rule: Stopping the To-Do List Virus

Step 8:   The Five-Minute Relationship Miracle

Step 9:   The Five-Minute Motivator

Step 10:   Self-Sabotage and Self-Belief

Step 11:   Avoiding Burnout and Overcommitment: "No" and the Personal Quota

Step 12:   Your Personal Power Hour

Step 13:   Have an Ugly Day

Step 14:   Giving Up the Cape

**Step 15:   Nightly Reflection: An Evening Routine to Nourish the
Soul and Transform Chaos to Centeredness**

*Prior to beginning this section please make sure you have completed
the Five Steps to a Successful Start in Part One.*

step 1

Meet the Catch-All Notebook (CAN)

"Rethink your approach ..." — *The theme for a series of Neutrogena print ads*

THE CAN QUIZ:

- Can you remember a time where you wrote an important note on the nearest piece of scrap paper...and it was never seen again?

- Can you remember a time when you wrote down what someone said so you wouldn't forget...only to forget where you wrote it down?

- Can you remember looking up (or asking for) the same phone number, address, or email multiple times?

- Can you remember a time when the adhesive on the back of an important sticky-note reminder gave out before the reminder was due?

- Can you recall a miscommunication that could have been avoided by writing something down?

- Can you remember having to phone someone to confirm an appointment because you misplaced the appointment card?

- Can you remember a time when you had a great idea and decided you could "write it down later" only to find the idea was long gone by then? Or you did write it down, but lost the piece of paper?

- Can you remember a time where you had so many to-do lists you couldn't find the current one?

Think about the childhood game of memory. A deck of cards is placed face down in a single layer and you take turns flipping over pairs with your opponent. When you match two cards you get to keep them. If the chosen cards do not match, you flip them back to their original position. When all the cards have been matched, the player with the most pairs wins. The larger the deck, the harder the challenge; even a small deck will have many adults flipping over unmatched pairs again and again.

This childhood game resembles how many of us try to manage day-to-day information. With memory alone people try to retain information and "flip over a match" on command. Those who do write things down often do so in multiple places, behind multiple tabs, and in order for a "match" to be found, the right place must be located (which is like playing several games of memory at one time).

One of the biggest myths of managing time, tasks, thoughts, reminders, and daily life is the belief that because our lives are com-plicated our systems must be complicated. I have tried keeping files for each day of the week, index systems, electronic information devices, and many other handy-dandy organizing gadgets, only to lose the Tuesday folder, accidentally send a note to school on the back of my Wednesday to-do card, or forget to change my batteries and lose all the information stored in my $500 foolproof gadget. I have owned a BlackBerry, a Treo, a Palm Pilot—you name it. Each time chaos came I assumed I must be using the wrong system. Perhaps a different size binder might work, or different tabs, or maybe the pretty pink paper would lure me to write everything down in its proper place.

All of these solutions worked brilliantly—for about two weeks. Then the magic wore off. One day as I sat amidst my piles of planners, realizing I had now run out of purchase options, I realized one of two statements must be true:

1. It was impossible for me to efficiently manage my day-to-day life.
2. These systems didn't match my needs.

Long ago I chose to remove the word "impossible" from my vocabulary; therefore I focused on the second statement.

I took an in-depth look at each abandoned solution, trying to figure out where the system had failed me. It didn't take long to draw some conclusions:

1. The system had way too many options for where to record my information.
2. The system did not provide enough room to keep all my daily thoughts and notes near my task items. Some days were blank, other days were overflowing.

What I needed was a simple system that could keep up with the daily demands of living. During a busy day, I don't have time to pick a tab, organize by due date or priority, or file a document behind the applicable letter. Without that time, I ended up jotting my notes on scratch paper. In addition, I needed something that wasn't too fancy. I needed something inviting to write in.

What I invented was the Catch-All Notebook (CAN). The CAN increases efficiency, maximizes time, and helps reduce stress — and it is simple. The CAN is a plain, lined notebook, small enough to accompany you everywhere. I use a five-by-seven-inch one-hundred-page spiral, but other women prefer both larger and smaller sizes. Choose what is most comfortable and portable for your life.

I have kept a notebook with me for as long as I can remember, but the "a-ha!" moment came when I began keeping the *same* notebook with me 24/7. Prior to that I cannot tell you how many notebooks I had floating around! I made life much more complicated by carrying around suitcase-sized systems whose cross-referencing could only be deciphered by a professional indexer.

Sound too simple? The secret of CAN's success is not the note-book, but how you use it.

CHOOSING YOUR CAN

All you need to start using this tool is a lined spiral notebook that is at least four-by-six inches in size. Make sure it will fit in your purse or whatever you carry daily. In about a week you will see why portability is vital.

Throughout the Toolbox we will be using index cards to rein-force important concepts, create checklists, and manage tasks. The self-adhesive pouches from the Getting Started Supply List should be adhered to your CAN to hold these cards. I have two pouches on both the front and back inside covers of my CAN.

Avoid choosing anything too fancy. Opt for plain and simple. We may resist writing or scribbling fast notes in fancy or expensive jour-nals because we do not want to "mess up" their pages. You don't need to go shopping: if you find notebooks around the house that are mostly blank, rip out the filled pages and use the rest as a CAN. (If you have kids in school, check their notebooks at the end of the year. Often they are one-quarter notes and three-quarters blank paper.)

Note: A bulky, tabbed planner or PDA is not a CAN. There are other uses for these in the program, but your CAN is a separate entity that functions in separate ways. If you keep a planner you could choose a size of CAN that fits in the planner, but when traveling without your planner you need to still keep your CAN with you. I know many people rely on computers and PDAs to store the majority of their information. They will not provide what we need for this Step — you still need to try the CAN.

WHAT DO I WRITE IN THE CAN?

In a nutshell—*everything*.

If I placed a photograph in front of you with one hundred objects and let you study it for three minutes before asking you to tell me everything you could remember, it would be challenging to recall one-tenth of the items.

If we repeated this exercise, and the second time you could write down objects and read the list back, your success rate would more than quadruple. The CAN offers the same effectiveness in your life. Here is an example of some items I found in my current CAN:

- Phone number for a local delivery restaurant, along with hours of delivery
- A page of meeting notes
- A grocery list
- A recipe for chili that a friend said I just had to try
- Due dates for bills I need to pay
- Something my daughter liked at the store that I might consider for birthday or Christmas
- Dates copied down from my church bulletin
- Appointments written down at the doctor (I no longer take the appointment cards)
- A variety of web sites I want to go back and visit when I have time
- The name of a book I saw on a television show
- The date and next step of a task I delegated to an employee
- A few notes about something that is bothering me and the start of some possible solutions
- A running list of to-do items
- The serial number for my Microsoft Ultimate 2007 upgrade
- Two ideas for essays along with some miscellaneous writing
- My word list while playing Boggle with my daughter

As you can see from this list, my CAN is a mirror of daily life. You can see actual sample pages (warning—they are messy!) online at www.brooknoelstudio.com.

CARDINAL CAN RULE: ANYWHERE YOUR BRAIN GOES THE CAN SHOULD GO TOO

We all have days where we feel our brains are elsewhere—but indeed they are with us 24/7. The CAN quickly becomes a spare brain and should be with us 24/7 too. People chuckle when I call it a "spare brain," but used correctly, that is exactly what it becomes. All the whirling thoughts in your mind are cleared into the CAN. Your mind is then left with room and energy to focus instead of spin. By having a functional notebook partner, you don't have to remember everything. Instead, you consult your trusted CAN. When distractions or worries relentlessly fill your mind, you record them in the CAN and reclaim your internal hard drive.

Common Questions:

Q. Do I take the CAN to bed with me?

A. While it need not join you in the bed, I do suggest placing it on your nightstand. Murphy's Law: as soon as you relax to the point of sleep you will think of something to write down. If you decide to "write it down in the morning," you may forget.

Q. Do I take the CAN with me when I go out for dinner?

A. Yes—if you take your brain, take your CAN. You can leave it in a purse, but do have it within arm's reach.

WHY IT WORKS

A while back I was reading through some neuroscience findings. The intent of the study was identifying common practices among high-functioning individuals. Keeping a notebook handy at all times to record passing thoughts, tasks, ideas and notes was an almost universal trait of the studied individuals, including Albert Einstein and Michaelangelo.

The research summarized three beneficial findings of this practice:

1. By keeping the notebook handy 24/7, it becomes a reliable location for confidently storing "mind matter." By transferring thoughts, tasks, ideas, and notes from mind to paper, the mind is free to focus on the task at hand.
2. The act of writing something down makes it more concrete and, statistically, increases the odds of remembering and accomplishing the written task.
3. By having all information accessible (within arm's reach) individuals are better able to maximize unexpected free time slots (even five to ten minutes).

WARNING: Do not make this more complicated than necessary by having separate notebooks — one for family matters, another for work matters, etc. Use only one notebook unless you are employed in a setting where corporate policy prohibits you taking any work notes out of the office. In that case, leave a work CAN on your desk. Take your personal CAN to work with you each day and set it out next to your work CAN. Place any notes or thoughts that are not work-related in the personal CAN that you keep with you at all times.

You may be wondering: *what about appointments and, and, and, and...?* The CAN is used to manage many active tasks, but before we add this feature, I encourage you to carry the CAN for twenty-four hours and begin writing down thoughts to get over the fear of "doing it right." Often we get so caught up in doing something the "right way," we don't do it all — which of course, is the wrong way! Since the CAN is a "reflection of your brain" whatever you write down is inherently correct.

In order to change anything, we need time and focus on our side. The CAN provides the foundation for both. When a builder begins a house, his focus is on the foundation, not the trim. The simple act of carrying the CAN and recording "mind-matter" for twenty-four hours provides a solid base for beginning this journey.

Carry the Catch-All-Notebook with you for
twenty four hours before proceeding.

ENHANCING THE CAN

That said, there are some "tricks of the trade" I want to share with you. Have your Catch-All Notebook handy so you can implement the instructions as you go along.

STARTING A CAN ENTRY

Draw a horizontal line at the bottom of your notes from the past twenty-four hours. Write today's date after the line. (Alternatively, you can start each day on a fresh page, although I prefer to just keep going and divide each day with a horizontal line.) Write the date in large letters or highlight it for easy reference.

ADDING ACTIVE TASKS

Active Tasks include any tasks you need to manage, work on, or complete *this week.* I consider the week to run Monday through Sunday, as Sunday afternoon is when I spend a half-hour completing my general planning for the week ahead. If needed, alter the week to match your lifestyle, for example Sunday to Saturday if Saturday would be the best day to do your planning. Don't have a planning routine? No problem. We create one in Step 15.

The first Active Task List you create will likely not contain a full week of tasks. Using my Monday to Sunday example, if I created my first Active Task List on a Thursday, I would only write down items to be completed on Thursday, Friday, Saturday, and Sunday. Then on Sunday I would "refresh" my Active Task List and add any tasks for the week to follow.

ACTIVE TASK LIST FAQ

Q. Do I write routine tasks like doing laundry or going grocery shopping on my Active Task List?

A. Think of the Active Task List as a cue card for life. If you are finding it challenging to complete a certain task effectively, write it on the list. Any tasks we complete effectively on "auto-pilot" need not go on the list. For example, brushing teeth does not need a "prompt," but if you have laundry piles needing attention this week, laundry would go on the list. If you have an effective laundry system already in place, there is no need to write it down. Generally it is easiest to keep household tasks separate. In the Housework Helpers Mini-Makeovers we set up a separate system for managing and maintaining the home.

Create your first Active Task List: Write down the action items for your first Active Task List before continuing.

ADDING A SHORT-TERM ACTION LIST

The Short Term Action List is used to manage or remember tasks that need attention within the next sixty days, but not this week. This is usually the longest list in the CAN. Use a paperclip, binder clip, or self-adhesive tab divider to mark a blank page approximately two-thirds into the notebook, leaving one-third of the notebook blank between the tab and back cover. Write Short Term Action List at the top of this page. Any time you think of tasks that need to be managed, completed, or remembered within this time frame, add them to this list. Since you will likely access this list often, the page marker provides quick access.

In order to manage any task effectively, the first step is to write it down (where we won't lose it). The first time you do this exercise it may take a while to write down all the Short-Term items. Or you may create an initial list and then find that ten more actions come to mind tomorrow. Don't worry—that is natural and will pass as you maintain this practice. Going forward you will have a workable list to manage.

SHORT TERM ACTION LIST FAQ

Q. Should I group my tasks by category? Put all your work tasks together, home tasks together, all child-related tasks together, etc.?

A. No. I strongly discourage this in the Catch-All Notebook. Most women find that adding multiple categories or lists creates too many choices to actively maintain the notebook or write each task in the correct place. While it may seem logical to group tasks by category, rarely do days progress "one category" at a time. More often than not we move back and forth between multiple types of tasks. The MTM program provides in-depth strategies for time management.

Add any items that come to mind to your Short-Term Action List before continuing.

LONG-TERM ACTION ITEMS

Long-Term Action Items are tasks needing attention more than sixty days from now. They do not get a list of their own in your Catch-All Notebook. The reason is simple: Choosing from three places to record information (Active, Short-Term and Long-Term) is too many. Remember, the Catch-All Notebook is meant to be an accessible daily companion, not a complicated or rigid system. In the hustle and bustle of daily life it would be unrealistic for most women to always choose the "right tab."

When we are busy it is unlikely we will pause and reflect: *hmmm… is this the optimal location for this task?* In reality, our thinking is much simpler: *Do I need to do this now or later?* The Active Task List is your "now." The Short-Term Action Items is the impending "later."

Using these two simple sections—Active or Short-Term—for recording tasks has proven to be a breakthrough for many women, because it matches how we think. Most planning systems are too complicated to match how we think during a busy day. We set up a detailed system only to find we write the wrong thing in the wrong place or can't find the specially marked tab.

That does not mean long-term tasks are abandoned. They do have a place to call their own, just not in the Catch-All Notebook. When you think of a task that is more than sixty days out, jot it down in your daily CAN notes and put a star next to it or the abbreviation "LT" for Long-Term.

Where I do put the Long-Term Tasks from Step One?

Since these are long term — more than sixty days out, they do not need to be processed daily. Once a month, or after your CAN is full (whichever comes first), transfer these notes or pages to the PLANNING tab in your Headquarters. Each time you create a new Short-Term envelope, check to see if any of these tasks have become Short-Term instead of Long-Term.

Another unique feature of the CAN is that it is undated. Have you ever set up a new planning or tracking system only to have your schedule change and need to rearrange all of your to-do items? The CAN avoids this date dilemma by keeping things simple: *do now* or *do next*.

Now that you have met your Catch-All Notebook, please join me in the CAN Pledge:

- I will no longer say "I don't need to write that down because I will remember it."
- I will no longer use sticky notes or other small papers with adhesive to jot down original notes, messages, and the like.
- I will no longer write on the nearest paper, envelope, or wrinkled corner of whatever is handy.
- I will no longer take a piece of valuable information from somewhere (i.e., business card, phone number) unless I first record it in my CAN or tape or staple the card to a page.
- I will no longer go anywhere without my CAN.

TAKE A STEP FORWARD

Each day we are constantly barraged with items to handle, address, reconcile or remember. Store these on paper, not in your head, and increase your focusing ability. Continue carrying your Catch-All Notebook with you EVERYWHERE.

Throughout the day, when a new to-do arises, add it to:

- The Active Task List if it will be completed this week.
- The Short-Term Action List if it will be completed within the next sixty days but not this week.

- Your general notes, thoughts, and ramblings of the day if it will be completed more than sixty days from now. Place a star or the abbreviation LT (for Long Term) next to it.

Use as many pages as needed each day.

TOOLS, RESOURCES, AND REFERENCES

- ☑ View sample pages of my Catch-All Notebook online.
- ☑ Stop in at the shop to browse our branded Catch-All Notebooks.

toolbox step 2

The Three-Step Action List

"The Constitution only guarantees the American people the right to pursue happiness. You have to catch it yourself."—*Benjamin Franklin*

Have you ever put something important aside, thinking you will begin tomorrow? Have you ever had a day where you were incredibly busy without a moment to spare, only to fall into bed and have no clue what you actually accomplished?

Many women have developed an addiction to "busyness." Try talking about how busy you are with a group, and undoubtedly another woman will overtake the conversation. "You think you are busy. I have to…" She then rattles off a list longer than Santa's on a good year. Many women have internalized a correlation between busyness and value or self-worth. The more we get done, the "better" we are.

Who would you rather be: the ragged woman racing to get the most done, or the balanced woman who knows that every day she has completed three things that matter?

The Three-Step Action List is a tool to help women maintain focus and take strides toward *what matters most* on a given day. While it sounds like a simple concept, many days we find our daily action items have little to do with our priorities. We get bogged down with "this and that" and forget we have the power to actively choose how we spend time and energy.

You are likely familiar with the priority planning systems in which items are coded A, B, or C based on importance. With a long list, however, labeling can become as complicated as completing a task! In addition, an item's priority may change after several days, and if we follow our previous rankings, we would overlook a task whose priority has increased. The Three-Step Action List allows us to hone in on current-day priorities, understanding that our life can change greatly from day to day.

In addition, to-do lists often become to-don't lists when they are overwhelming and long. We create confusion and chaos when we try to focus on twenty tasks in a single day all clamoring for energy and attention. Notice this list is called *Three*-Step Action List (not five or ten or twenty). Most days you will find you can easily cross off all three items and move on to other things. It's much more gratifying to complete three and go back for more, rather than starting off with a long list.

The Three-Step Action List helps…

1. To keep us focused and avoid spinning our wheels.
2. To have a sense of accomplishment each day instead of feeling we didn't get enough done and/or having a load of guilt on our shoulders.
3. To keep us energized. Tackling three items isn't overwhelming—when we do ten or twenty or more, we can quickly burnout on to-do items.

GUIDELINES FOR CREATING A THREE-STEP ACTION LIST:

What you choose to place on this list is entirely up to you. You can choose routine tasks or non-routine tasks. You can choose three items from your CAN's Active Task List. The only necessity is for one of the three action items to move you forward in the Life Area at the top of your Action Plan.

TIPS FOR SUCCESS:
*   Do not complicate the Three-Step Action List tool by trying to create one list for work, one for family, one for personal—

doing so quickly brings you back to a large list of to-dos that defeats the purpose. While many items vie for attention each day, prioritizing the three most important allows effective focus without becoming sidetracked. After completing three, you can always go back for more.

- Most people do best with a list created the night before. This discourages us from changing plans at the last minute.
- Choose tasks that can be realistically completed in a single day—even with interruptions. The goal is to choose three tasks that will allow you to feel positive come evening—even if nothing else goes as planned during the day. How long an action takes to complete has no bearing on whether it should be on the list or not. Sometimes your lists may contain all items that can be done in five minutes or less. Other times you may have longer tasks. On days where you have a more time-consuming action item, try to keep the other two items smaller.
- Make sure your steps are tasks—not projects. A project requires multiple steps. A task requires a single step. Break projects down into tasks and place only tasks on your Three-Step Action List.
- Three-Step Action Lists can contain items from your Active Task List, Short-Term Task List, or Long-Term Action Items.
- Use the Three-Step Action List every day. If you are on vacation, choose three actions that help maximize the vacation day. If you are sick, choose three actions that will help you recover (rest, fluids, etc.).

If you do not implement the Three-Step Action List, you will likely find yourself in the exact same place you are today six months from now. W.L. Bateman said, "If you keep on doing what you've always done, you'll keep on getting what you've always got." If you don't want to keep getting what you've got, implement this tool wholeheartedly.

TAKE A STEP FORWARD

Imagine meeting up with a friend with whom you have not connected in a long while. This friend asks you what you have been up to over the past year. You respond, "Many things—in fact over a thousand things that moved me toward my goals. How about you?"

While three actions might seem a small list, over time it adds up quickly, ultimately yielding an end result that far surpasses the standard to-do list. Tuck the Super-Woman Cape in the off-season clothes and begin using the Three-Step Action List. I guarantee you will get more done (and more of the *right* stuff done, the *right* way) than trying to accomplish twenty daily tasks. Each day when you create your new CAN entry, write your Three-Step Action List below the date for easy reference throughout the day. If you finish all three tasks, then and only then, you can go back and add more after giving yourself a pat on the back.

TOOLS, RESOURCES, AND REFERENCES
⊠ Share your Three-Step Action List online in the Three-Step Database or join in the Three-Step Daily Discussion board
⊠ Print copies of the Three-Step Action List index card for colorful reminders and place inside a CAN self-adhesive pocket.

toolbox step 3

How Do You Start Your Day?

"Something great is going to happen today… I can't wait to see what it is!" —*Brook Noel*

Studies have shown that breakfast is the most important meal of the day. It affects our energy level, metabolism, focus ability, and health. Undoubtedly, the first fuel of the day for the body is very important. Equally important is the first emotional fuel for the mind. Imagine this scene with me:

The alarm goes off, and you struggle to get out of bed on time as the electronic beeping pierces your eardrum. Your first thought is, "When is daylight savings?" How you would love the extra hour. Remembering daylight savings happened last weekend, you sigh, stumble to your feet, and head toward the shower.

After showering and dressing you go downstairs to find your family at the breakfast table. "Good morning," you say as enthusiastically as possible at 6:00 a.m.. You are greeted with a few moments of silence, then a half-hearted "hello" before everyone returns to his or her breakfast bowls and conversation. You grab a cup of coffee and a muffin to have on your way to work.

While driving to work your cell phone rings. It is one of your closest friends. After a cursory hello, she breaks into an auctioneer ramble. "I'm really in a jam. My babysitter called, and she is sick. Can you watch my kids tonight for thirty minutes while I run and pick up Jacob's present?" Always there for one another, you tell her you would be happy to watch the kids, before hanging up the phone.

*You get to work and find someone in your designated parking place. Frustrated, your "okay mood" is drastically deteriorating. You park near the back of the lot only to step into a wad of gum as you get out of the car. "UGH," you think, "it's going to be one of **those** days."*

You shuffle into the office, passing the receptionist. Normally she welcomes you with a cheerful greeting, but today she is busy taking notes while talking on the phone and doesn't offer so much as a nod. You sigh again and plod to the meeting room.

Any idea what is missing in this scene?

Two simple words: GOOD MORNING (backed by sincerity and enthusiasm). *The first thirty to sixty minutes of our day set the tone for the hours to come. Your emotional fuel in the morning has a dramatic impact on how the day flows and unfolds.*

Have you noticed that people who complain about bills and debt seem to get further into debt?

Have you noticed that people who complain and are negative tend to have more negative things happen than their noncomplaining counterparts?

Have you ever noticed that people who have seemingly boundless energy and optimism have something new and wonderful to report almost every time you visit?

Have you noticed that people who frequently complain or degrade themselves about their weight tend to fail in weight loss endeavors?

Are you detecting a trend? Good. Let's transfer this trend to Good Morning.

I want you to stop for a moment and visualize the last thirty days. How did your mornings start? What was happening during the first hour after you awoke?

I am not psychic, but I am going to go out on a limb and make a few predictions:

If you began most of your days thinking negatively (life is too stressful; I am overwhelmed; I have too much to do), I would predict that your month has been stressful, you feel overwhelmed, and you haven't gotten much done.

If you began most of your days thinking very positively (something great will happen today; I like myself; I am so grateful that I have food and/or shelter and/or health), I would predict that your days, for the most part, were content and fulfilling, and you had unexpected moments of joy.

If you began your days somewhere in the middle of the two examples above (or just on autopilot), I would venture to say that your month probably looked a lot like the month before—no significant change, certainly not for the better.

Eleanor Roosevelt said, "Whether you think you can or think you can't, you're right." Most women who come to the Challenge are here because we know we deserve more, and we know we can have a richer, fuller life—we just need a path to follow.

A proper Good Morning is an essential component of that path. You could implement every Step in this program, but without a Good Morning you will be missing a vital tool for content and balanced living.

Thousands of women have confirmed the value of starting their day with the simple statement, "Something great is going to happen today, I can't wait to see what it is!" Children have joined their mothers in saying "Good Morning," and husbands have too. One boy painted, "Something great is going to happen today," on the side of his float for a local parade. Workplaces post my daily Good Morning newsletter where all employees can see it each day. This affirmation, coupled with a few minutes of positive intention, can quickly change the tone of a day, a week, a month, a life.

Life might happen on its own, but we are the ones who steer our hearts and minds. If you don't actively steer, don't act surprised when you wind up somewhere you don't want to be. Let today be the last day you live on autopilot. It's time to take the wheel.

TAKE A STEP FORWARD

Tomorrow when you wake up, do not jump into a crazy pace. Take the time for the crucial step of saying hello to yourself. Before even getting out of bed, take a few deep breaths, and say "Good morning."

Say a quick prayer. Focus on your day ahead, and imagine moving through it effortlessly. While getting dressed, develop curiosity about the day. Try saying, "I know something great will happen today...I can't wait to see what it is." It might be awkward at first, but stick with it. Create reminders on blank index cards and put them by your alarm clock or mirror so you remember this Step upon waking.

Days, homes, and work environments have been transformed through Good Mornings. Let your positive transformation begin tomorrow morning.

TOOLS, RESOURCES, AND REFERENCES
- ☑ Visit my Good Morning blog to read a new Good Morning inspiration each day or sign up to receive Good Morning messages by email. www.brooknoelstudio.com/goodmorning/
- ☑ Listen online or download a free mp3 audio of my "Monday Morning with Brook Noel" inspirational message.
- ☒ Print copies of the "Good Morning" prompt cards, and add one to your CAN until this becomes a habit.
- ☒ Download and print the *Good Morning: Twenty Inspirations to Begin Your Day* e-book to have inspirational reading within arm's reach.
- ☒ Visit the Inspirations library for audio downloads.

toolbox step 4

The Catch-It Collectors

"Consider the postage stamp; its usefulness consists in the ability to stick to one thing until it gets there."—*Josh Billings*

Time and time again I hear from women who find managing day-to-day paper to be a significant stressor. This isn't surprising given the amount of paper we acquire in the course of a day. I created the Catch-It Concept as a tool for overcoming the paper pile problem.

The sole purpose of the Catch-It Envelopes created in this Step is to deal with *new incoming paper* effectively and avoid creating more piles. These envelopes place you in control of incoming paper, versus letting it control you.

CREATING YOUR CATCH-IT COLLECTORS

To corral new incoming paper effectively we need two types of Catch-It Envelopes, one set optimized for paper you acquire while outside the four walls of your home, and one set for the paper brought into your home, or delivered to your door by others. Let's start with the envelopes designed for paper outside the home.

OUTSIDE CATCH-IT ENVELOPES

If a lot of paper enters your life each day (or you acquire paper that cannot be folded) use a 9 x 12-inch paper envelope. For less paper, try a 6 x 9-inch envelope. I keep a large envelope in my purse (I carry a big purse that can even fit my mini-laptop). One of my employees keeps a receipt-sized envelope in her purse and a larger envelope in her car, since she doesn't regularly carry a big bag or large purse. She uses the purse envelope for receipts and puts all other papers in the envelope kept in the car.

Write "Catch It" in big letters on the front or choose a colored envelope you can easily distinguish from other envelopes. Cut out the clock illustration on page 63 and paste it to the front of the envelope or draw your own. **Note:** Don't write "time" or "clock," actually paste or draw the clock on the Outside Catch-It Envelope.

SUMMARY OF THE OUTSIDE CATCH-IT ENVELOPE

This envelope catches all the miscellaneous paper that enters your life while you are *outside of your home,* for example: receipts, free stuff you pick up, or paper someone gives you. Instead of stuffing these papers in your purse (which I am guessing you periodically clean out, throwing those papers into a pile), or throwing them into the backseat or visor of the car (which I am guessing you periodically clean out, throwing those papers in a pile), or stuffing them into a tote bag or briefcase (which I am guessing you periodically clean out, throwing those papers into a pile), you place them in this envelope.

From this day forward, the Outside Catch-It Envelope should accompany you whenever you leave the home. This practice encourages selectivity—you will likely find yourself naturally

---

Why is there a clock on the envelope? Everything that makes its way into this Outside Catch-It Envelope will, in one way or another, require your time. Even throwing something out later requires time.

Most people report lack of free time as one of their biggest life stressors. (If you did have free time, would you want to spend it reading or sorting through free informational brochures?) This clock acts as a constant reminder that what goes into that envelope will undoubtedly consume your time.

thinking twice about adding a free magazine or informational brochure from the doctor's office if you have to cart it around all day and then sort it at night—which is what we implement in the daily processing and Nightly Reflection in Step 15.

THE IN-HOUSE CATCH-IT COLLECTORS

While the Outside Catch-It Envelope collects paper acquired outside of the home, we still need a solution for the paper others bring or deliver to our home. Permission slips, completed school papers, warranties from opened packages, non-junk mail, and informational brochures are a few examples of paper in this category.

Since most women also manage the majority of house-paper, it is important to have a designated area for family members to deliver incoming information. Without a designated "home," these papers are often lost in the shuffle. A family member may set an important document needing your attention on a counter and then wonder *where you put it.* Likewise, if you acquire new paper such as non-junk mail or a warranty inside a package while in the home, a designated "paper collector" avoids creating stressful piles or lost documents.

I used a wire basket as an inbox until I discovered a major problem. An open basket can be piled as high as gravity-building skills allow. Once a pile is created, the system becomes inefficient because it takes too long to find anything. I have found three-sided vertical storage to be much more effective for two reasons:

1. Vertical storage separates this paper from piles
2   Being three-sided, it has a built-in paper limit

VERTICAL STORAGE OPTIONS AND SUGGESTIONS

Magnetic Holders: When I used to process my paper two or three times per week, I attached a magnetic holder to the fridge. Most office supply stores stock magnetic paper-sized organizers.

Job Jackets: When I switched to daily processing I switched to a smaller collector. I use a dual-pocket job jacket or pocket. These pockets are used as job ticket holders in many warehouses, making them a durable choice for handling a busy life! These are available with the wide opening at the top or bottom, in single-pocket or dual-pocket formats, and with a hole at the top for easy hanging. Most hold about fifty sheets effectively.

My family members place any paper intended for me in the large pocket. Then any information I am returning to my husband or daughter, goes into the front pocket; for example, a permission slip or list.

Paper Envelopes: While I like vinyl job jackets for durability, any paper envelope will do the trick. Place the envelope upright on a frequently passed counter using bookends or knick-knacks, or hang it from the fridge with a couple of strong-hold magnet clips.

PLACING THE IN-HOME CATCH-IT COLLECTORS

Place the In-Home Collector as near to the front door as possible to ensure family members pass it regularly. If you use a coat closet, hang it next to the coat closet or on the backside of the closet door. Let family members know this is the new destination for any incoming paper. I was fairly straightforward telling my husband that if it didn't go in the collector I was not responsible for its whereabouts. Since he would prefer me to be responsible, he adapted quite quickly.

HELPING THE FAMILY ADAPT

Family members will likely forget to use the in-home envelope at first, so use these strategies to guide them along.

1. When they go to hand you something, ask that they place it inside the envelope.
2. If they ask if you have seen a paper, reply with "Did you put that in my envelope?" If they say "no," then reply you have not seen it.
3. Put anything they need back from you in the "out" envelope—lunch money, checks, etc. This will help them get used to checking the envelope.

ADAPTATION IDEAS FOR LARGER FAMILIES

Families of five or more likely need a bit more space to avoid everything being crammed in together or having "outbound" papers confused. The simplest solution is to use color. Both paper envelopes and jackets come in many colors. If using the jackets, hang on the backside of a door at different heights.

If you are using paper envelopes, have one or two envelopes for your incoming items and then provide a different colored envelope for each family member's returned items. Place vertically near the front door (if you have an entryway table) or on a frequently passed counter.

WHY NOT FILES OR IN-BASKETS?

Over the past two years, I have abandoned files, paper-sorters, and inboxes. I have replaced these with envelopes or other three-sided-storage. While wire baskets, in-baskets, file folders, and paper stackers are marketed as "paper-organizers," for me they are paper-pile-enablers. Most women find that these products quickly become a tool for creating organized piles, not action systems. As simple as envelopes are, they have some very unique qualities which make them the number one choice for action systems:

The Sides are Sealed: Unlike manila folders where paper can sneak out at every edge, an envelope provides a "container" solution.

Natural Paper Limit: An open basket can be piled as high as gravity-building skills allow. Envelopes have a built-in limit.

Stand Up for Storage: They are easy to store: instead of creating piles, envelopes can be stored upright for easy viewing.

Practical and Portable: Envelopes create an easy-reference system for finding the information you need quickly. Need to pay bills? Grab the bills envelope.

Important Reminder:

Please remember the Catch-It Tools created in this Step are only for NEW incoming paper entering your life from this day forward. Leave all of your existing paper alone – don't sneak it into these envelopes or they will be filled before you begin. We are focused on stopping the problem going forward. Dealing with paper backlog is best done with my Paper Piles strategies. (You can learn more at the website.)

TAKE A STEP FORWARD

Create your Outside Catch-It Envelope and the Inside Catch-It Collectors. In Step 15, we implement the Nightly Reflection and cover how to process this paper and integrate the Steps you have learned so far into an effective daily planning and management system.

toolbox step 5

Moments of Magic

"The real voyage of discovery consists not in seeking new landscapes, but in having new eyes."—*Marcel Proust*

Have you ever multitasked while watching a comedy with your family? Do you then become so absorbed in the task at hand that you miss something in the movie? Everyone in the room laughs or gasps, and you then realize you were so engrossed in what you were doing that you completely missed "the moment." At this point you likely ask someone to fill you in or you try to catch up on your own. Either way, this example demonstrates how focus influences our experience.

If we could rewind time and look at the entire room through a monitoring camera, we would find that everyone in the room was exposed to the same sounds. The television was on, a movie was playing, and there were X people in the room. Then, all of the people laughed except for one—even though everyone was exposed to the same audio. The person who did not laugh had tuned it out, and therefore experienced a different emotion than the others. This explains how two people can often experience the same thing but recount it quite differently. While they were both in the same place at the same time their focus was different, and *this different focus created a different reality.*

From moment to moment, we control where we direct our focus. Is our ten-day vacation half-over already or do we have five wonderful days left? Either answer is correct, but one also creates joy. If we do not step in and take direction of our focus, it will remain on autopilot. Life will move forward, but we will not be an active participant in directing its course. Living on autopilot creates days, weeks, months, and years of missing magical moments.

I became aware of this principle during an overscheduled day in 1997, when my daughter was a toddler with her own agenda. I wrote this "Cherish Your Wood Chips" essay later that day.

CHERISH YOUR WOOD CHIPS

Today was one of those days in which I just couldn't get enough done. No matter how many times my pen scratched off a to-do list item, a new one seemed to appear. But you, Samantha, didn't have anything on your agenda. At sixteen months, your days are usually quite free.

I sat in my home office, routinely punching computer keys, and you came to my office door. You had your coat, draped over your head, looking like a little green goblin.

"Samantha, we can't go outside today. For one, it's cold, and secondly, I just have too much on my plate." One of your blue eyes peered out questioningly from beneath the green cape. You then walked to the door and pounded on it. I realized that working was futile—you wanted to go play.

I glanced at my watch. If we hurried, we could be back in thirty minutes, enough time to satiate your needs for the outside world without interfering with my needs on the inside world.

Together, hand in hand, we walked down to the park. I was ready to take you on your favorite swing. Instead, you plopped down in a pile of wood chips. I watched, half in amazement and half in frustration, as you scrutinized each one. Turning it. Tasting it. Feeling it.

I let out a sigh and situated myself on a low monkey bar. *I don't have time for this,* I thought. I didn't say the words, but Samantha, I had brought you here to swing. I had brought you here to play. And since you were just examining wood chips, I thought of the ways this time could be better spent. My to-do list ran through my mind:

change the laundry, answer email, finish pre-pub issue, respond to Eric's galleys, finish Ken's marketing campaign, send kit to Scholastic.

I let out another sigh and was about to pick you up and take you home, when a little boy approached. I watched as you excitedly ran to him. You displayed each proud find, each beautiful wood chip.

The little boy smiled like it was a holiday as he accepted each offering. When your hands were empty, you ran back for more.

The boy continued to smile. He was with his grandmother, and while she paused for your sixty-second exchange, she then hustled him along saying, "We need to get on the swing so I can get back and finish dinner."

You watched the boy on the swing. It was like a silent communication. You knew that he, too, would rather be playing with the wood chips.

After about ten minutes on the swing and a few glances at her watch, the grandmother caught the young boy and began the descent home. Your gaze followed him—Samantha, you don't have a poker face—and you were sad. You plopped back into the wood chips and began to pick them up again. One by one. You had no dinner to fix. You weren't even hungry. The only thing of importance was the wood chips and someone else who could understand their magnificence.

I was saddened a bit as I watched you there. Eventually you will have dinner to cook, you might have your own kids to take to the park, laundry to do, or a boss to reckon with. Somewhere, somehow, you will learn the constraints of our world. But not today.

As I watched you, I realized I could be like the grandmother and pull you from the magic land of wood chips and take you back to the world of time and accountability. But in that instant, I knew I needed those wood chips too.

So I went down next to you. I on my back, in light-colored clothes, immersed in a pile of wet, muddy wood chips; you in your jeans, kneeling, intently handing me each one.

We made the chips into a necklace. We built them into a tower. We stuck them down our shirts. We played catch with them. We pretended they were pizza. We imagined what they would say if they could speak. We smiled at them and pretended that they smiled back.

People mulled around the park, taking their dogs for ten-minute walks, skipping along on their thirty-minute jogs. I am sure they thought we were crazy.

When I next glanced at my watch, two hours had passed. We both had wood chips in our hair and mud on our clothes, but I don't think either of us has ever looked more beautiful.

You stood up, ready now, to go home. And I took your hand and we walked together.

When we got home, I took out a pen and paper and in big black lettering I wrote: "Cherish Your Wood Chips." I stuck it in my daily planner, right across from my to-do list.

Samantha, when I woke up this morning, I didn't know you would hand me one of the secrets to happiness. When I awoke this morning, I did not understand the value of a wood chip.

CREATING MAGICAL MOMENTS

Reflect for a moment on whatever you have done thus far today:

- Did you have coffee this morning? If so, were you aware of what cup you chose? Did you choose your favorite cup? Write down your answer. Then think about tomorrow morning. Is there something you can do differently that brings a simple pleasure and awareness to your morning?

- When you passed someone or a pet you cared for today, did you tell them so? Is there something you can do differently tomorrow that brings simple pleasure and awareness?

- Look at what you are wearing. Is it an outfit that makes you feel good? Did you pick it because you like it? Did you add any accessories? Is there something you can do differently tomorrow that brings simple pleasure and awareness?

- When out and about did you open the door for a stranger or genuinely converse with someone who assisted you while shopping? Is there something you can do differently tomorrow that brings simple pleasure and awareness?
- Did you drive a car today or ride a bus or public transport? If so, what were you reading or listening to? Did you take a positive book? A favorite CD? Is there something you can do differently tomorrow that brings simple pleasure and awareness?
- When you stepped outside today did you pause for a moment to look around and be thankful or see a tree or cloud or star you may not have noticed before? Is there something you can do differently tomorrow that brings simple pleasure and awareness?

The answers to these questions reveal opportunities to find pleasure all around us. Magic doesn't require a genie in a bottle — it requires awareness. Use your answers to these questions to increase positive awareness and make magic tomorrow.

TAKE A STEP FORWARD

Tomorrow, look for opportunities to create joy. In your journal or on an index card, record how you create joy. When I started this practice I "checked-in" at the top of the hour. If I hadn't created a positive moment, then I created one at that time. After a couple of months I no longer needed the index card as I was uncovering magical moments at every turn. Continue the written practice until you find your perspective transforming into one in which positive and magical moments become a regular occurrence. If you choose index cards, date and save the cards to reflect on throughout the year.

toolbox step 6

Soul Food: Creating a Personal Power Deck

"Watch your thoughts, for they become words. Choose your words, for they become actions. Understand your actions, for they become habits. Study your habits, for they will become your character. Develop your character, for it becomes your destiny."—*Frank Outlaw*

I have always been a "quote collector." Even as a child, my allowance funds were spent on inspirational wallet cards at the local bookstore. Just after college, I started a "Quote Collection" in a beautiful blank book I had received for Christmas. With my best penmanship (which isn't so great) I would write phrases, sentences, or paragraphs that resonated with me. Whenever I needed a pick-me-up I would turn to these inspiring and encouraging words. As the years went by, I started adding my own affirmations, favorite memories, and kind emails or letters. During times of stress, emotional letdown, or discontentment, I would turn to this wellspring of rejuvenation. Each time I turned the pages, I found inspiration and encouragement.

Years later I began adding a daily dose of this "Soul Food" to my life. I experimented with many ways to digest these nuggets of wisdom. Ultimately I decided the book wasn't a practical means of delivery. This daily dose of Soul Food needed to be portable, not a bulky book. We don't eat all our food for the day at breakfast time because we can't digest it, store it, and it would fail to fuel us throughout the day. Soul Food works the same way. We can't read a positive book or quote in the morning and expect the effects to last all day. In order to achieve optimal emotional health, we need Soul Food regularly throughout the day.

I transformed my quote book into a Soul Food *Personal Power Deck* and for over a decade I have reaped the benefits. These cards are fun, easy, and rewarding to make. I love watching women leave my workshops with a Soul Food Box packed with cards. The concept has been so well-received that I have created free printable cards as well as a complete Soul Food: Personal Power Deck with thirty-six cards to accompany the CYLC and MTM programs.

HOW TO BUILD YOUR PERSONAL POWER DECK

CYLC-MADE CARDS
I have designed several printable cards to start your deck. Each starter card features a quote or question set against my original artwork. You can print these out at http://www.brooknoelstudio.com

SELF-MADE CARDS
Keep an eye out for inspiring quotes, affirmations, song lyrics, compliments, sentences from books, or lines from a movie or show. Write these nuggets down in your CAN, or on the inside cover. Regularly transfer your inspirations to index cards. If you aren't pleased with your penmanship, type your messages on computer, print, and then cut and tape or paste onto index cards.

Get Inspired Online

The internet provides a wealth of quote resources. A few of my favorites include:

www.quotegarden.com
www.thinkexist.com
www.quoteworld.org

GROUP CARDS

If you are working on the *Challenge* within a small group, ask each group participant to bring a new card to each meeting, or allot fifteen minutes per meeting for card making. Mix the cards together and let each participant pick a card to take home.

A note for those who want to get fancy...

With the popularity of paper arts, from collage to card-making to scrapbooking and beyond, many women have papers, stamps, stickers, and more on-hand. Use your paper-art techniques to enhance your cards. If you aren't a paper-arts enthusiast or consider yourself uncreative, you can still easily enhance your cards. Visit a craft, scrapbook, or stamp store for inspiration galore. A few decorative stickers and decorative paper sheets last for many cards.

TAKE A STEP FORWARD

Pick up some plain index cards or cut cardstock or paper into three-by-five-inch squares. Try your hand at a few Personal Power Cards. If you are stuck for ideas, use some of the quotes found at the opening of each Step. Insert a Soul Food Card into a self-adhesive pocket within your CAN.

TOOLS, RESOURCES, AND REFERENCES

- ☑ View my quote collection online and links to other inspirational quote websites.
- ☑ Get your deck started easily with the three Personal Power Cards I have made for you.
- ☑ Visit our online shop to learn more about the MTM make-your-own Personal Power Deck kit that includes supplies, cards, and suggestions. Or browse the selection of ready-made Personal Power Cards.

☒ While working through the program, watch for interactive checklists. After completing an interactive checklist online you will receive a printable Personal Power Card reward.

☒ Share pictures of your Personal Power Cards and view other member cards in the Inspirations area.

toolbox step 7

The Five-Minute Rule:
Stopping the To-Do List Virus

"Don't say you don't have enough time. You have exactly the same number of hours per day that were given to Helen Keller, Pasteur, Michelangelo, Mother Teresa, Leonardo da Vinci, Thomas Jefferson, and Albert Einstein." —*H. Jackson Brown, Jr.*

My friend Sara shared this simple Step that, when practiced routinely, will dramatically increase your effectiveness.

> *The Five-Minute Rule: If something can be done in five minutes or less — DO IT NOW! Don't add it to your To-Do list. It will take more time and energy to write down, manage, and keep thinking about than it will take to get it done.*

Here are some examples of how this can be applied:

Either answer the phone or don't. If you are intensely involved in or focused on a project, then either turn off your phone or silence the ringer. If you are expecting a call or need to take calls, then keep a phone by you. Instead of glancing down at caller ID and answering only if it is someone you want to talk to, use these criteria: if the call length would be around five minutes, and not answering creates a call you need to return, answer the phone instead. Your flow has already been interrupted by the ring and glancing at the phone to identify the caller. If you answer and talk for five minutes, you avoid…

1. Needing to remember to call the person back
2. Writing the call on your to-do list

3. Deciding when to call the person back
4. Moving the item around on your to-do list if you don't feel like doing it
5. Wondering about what the caller wants
6. The stress of another to-do

Mail: If you have something you need to mail, instead of thinking about mailing it or putting it in a pile "to mail," find an envelope and address it. Print stamps on www.stamps.com or have a roll handy. Add a stamp. Walk to your mailbox, place it inside, and put the flag up so the postal delivery person knows to pick it up.

When I put this rule into practice I was amazed by how many things could actually be done in five minutes or less. I can empty and refill the dishwasher in five minutes or less. I can fold a load of laundry and start a new load in five minutes or less. I can rinse and slice up fresh fruit for a nutritious salad in five minutes or less. I can walk a half mile in five minutes or less. The list goes on...

TAKE A STEP FORWARD
Start using the Five-Minute Rule tomorrow. Watch how quickly your to-do list changes with its implementation.

toolbox step 8

The Five-Minute Relationship Miracle

"They may forget what you said, but they will never forget how you made them feel." —*Carl W. Buechner*

Years ago, after a communication workshop, I was talking to the presenter about listening. Somewhere within the conversation he asked if I was a good listener. I exclaimed, "Of course!" He then asked, "Do you know what time it is?"

I glanced at my watch. "6:00 p.m."

"Nope," he answered confidently.

I looked down at my watch and then back to the speaker. "Then your watch must be wrong," I replied.

He glanced at his silver watch. "No my, watch also says 6:00 p.m."

"Then how is what I said inaccurate?"

"I didn't ask you *what time* it was. I asked if you *knew* what time it was."

I smiled, realizing what was *actually asked* and what I *actually heard* were two different things—and I even had reason to be on the lookout since he was a communications expert.

If we do not hone our listening ability, we will face miscommunications that could have otherwise been prevented. While we can hear many things simultaneously—a car, a bird, music, a person speaking—we cannot *listen* to all of these sounds simultaneously. Hearing is passive, listening is active.

Any time a person interrupts, she is not listening. If she were listening she would be waiting to hear all that is said to ensure she responds accordingly. Interruptions signal an assumption has been made about what the speaker is saying. Because this assumption has been made, the person interrupts and begins their response. Yet, how can we know what someone is going to say if they haven't said it? We might have clues—a person's posture, history, tone— but that doesn't mean a banana can ride a skateboard. Caught you, didn't I? What you anticipated that sentence would read and what it actually read were two different things. If you had assumed this paragraph would flow logically because the others paragraphs have, your assumption would be wrong.

If I do not listen to you, I cannot fully respond to you. If I cannot fully respond to you, you cannot fully respond to me. If we cannot fully respond to one another, we cannot communicate in a healthy, fulfilling way because neither of us ever truly heard one another. Instead, we heard what we thought each other was saying, and we responded to thoughts versus words.

The Academy-Award nominated movie *Babel* had a great tagline: "If you want to be understood, seek first to understand." The Five-Minute Relationship Miracle can help you do just that.

The Five-Minute Relationship Miracle has the ability to dramatically improve any relationship. Relatives, spouse, children, colleagues, and friends—all will appreciate this focused connection in an age in which people often multitask while talking or hear without listening. Here's how it works:

1. Each day, choose a relationship you feel would benefit from a focused connection.
2. For five minutes, give that person your total attention. What does that mean?
   a. **Stop multitasking:** Do not do this while washing the dishes, wiping down the counter, filing papers, sorting mail, unpacking groceries, etc.

b. **Listen only to him or her:** Do not get caught up in your own thoughts, or think ahead about how you will respond; just listen.

c. **See them as they are:** Do not project traits, qualities, or your needs. Avoid having an agenda or goal. The richness of communication comes through letting go of preconceived notions, our own needs, and our own expectations. See this person as he or she is and let that be enough.

d. **Use nonverbal communication:** Ninety percent of communication is nonverbal. Use touch where appropriate, maintain eye contract, lean forward, and uncross your arms.

Many people have racing minds and may find it challenging to achieve this level of focus. As someone with Attention Deficit Disorder (ADD), I can definitely relate. One technique I have found helpful is silently repeating what is said in my mind. At first I had to do this for the entire five-minute period. Soon I was able to maintain focus without using this technique for the full five minutes. I still keep it in my toolbox though, and use it whenever I find my mind wandering. After silently repeating a couple of sentences of the conversation, my focus naturally returns.

If you are struggling with this Step after applying the silent-repeat technique, build up to five minutes over time. Start with one or two minutes, then add a half minute or a minute at a time until you reach the five-minute goal.

TAKE A STEP FORWARD

Apply the Five-Minute Relationship Miracle daily to the relationship of your choice. (You can work on the same relationship each day for a period of time, or work on a different relationship daily.) This tool works with friends, children, relatives, significant others, colleagues, doctors—it will be hard to find someone who does not appreciate or respond positively in this age of distraction.

Remember, the more you use this tool the more you will enrich your relationships.

toolbox step 9

The Five-Minute Motivator

"Our real problem is not our strength today; it is rather the vital necessity of action today to ensure our strength tomorrow." —*Calvin Coolidge*

Delaying, procrastinating, and doing it later are common practices in today's hectic world. Some live by the motto, "If I wait until the last minute, it only takes a minute," while others find themselves distracted by other happenings or lack of motivation. When action-delays repeatedly occur, the "Do-It-Later" habit often develops. This habit is easy to maintain because it is socially acceptable and shared by the masses.

The Do-It-Later habit has similarities to a coffee habit. Coffee is addictive. I am having a cup right now. I doubt anyone is going to storm into my home and conduct an intervention because I am clutching a mug of French Roast. Actually, if a group of people stormed in, I would likely serve coffee. We might all agree that drinking green tea, water, or orange juice is a better and healthier action, but drinking coffee is acceptable. Likewise the Do-it-Later habit is acceptable because so many people are doing it and perceive breaking the habit to be too challenging to accomplish.

If we try to change a behavior that is not socially acceptable (excessive drinking, smoking, binge eating, drugs), support mechanisms abound. From hotlines to support groups to hospitals to sponsors, many people are ready to help. But many people face a challenge that is much more subtle and quiet. We *face the challenge of knowing we can improve, achieve, and "become more" — we just can't quite figure out how to get out of our own way long enough to do so.*

ADDICTED TO CHANGE

Bundled with the Do-it-Later habit is another addiction — Change Addiction. The markets of self-help, diet, and fitness have experienced an incredible boom over the past decade. Perhaps you have found yourself visiting an all-too-familiar self-help shelf again and again. Some of the books are gems; many are not. Most lead us back to the same shelf sooner rather than later. Yet we return because while we carry the book to the register, or wait for it to arrive in the mail, we have a feeling of hope.

Maybe you have ordered an ab cruncher, twister, or rotator because it came with a guarantee of results in two to four weeks. Perhaps a weight-loss solution caught your attention — you may have seen a tiny television spokesperson pull out the waistband on old pants that could now fit three, telling you the astronomical number of pounds that you could lose in just a week's time. Maybe a newsstand magazine captured your interest with a headline about "Getting Organized in Five Easy Steps," or "Save Hundreds on Your Grocery Bill," or "Find the Man of Your Dreams this Year," or "Lose a Dress Size by the Weekend."

Can you relate to any of these examples? If so, you are among friends. Many people seek out these solutions; otherwise the industry would not be booming. The majority of these solutions must fail — otherwise why would we see such growth? How many Mr. Right's do you need to find? How many times do you need to lose a hundred pounds?

Many of these "solutions" share some of these common features:

1. Thousands upon thousands of dollars have gone into packaging, sales, and marketing created by experts to tap into our core needs.

2. While the plan might work, the level of action required is unrealistic for all but a select few.
3. The "promise" is a quick solution, which appeals to our overtaxed schedule.
4. The solution is too complicated to figure out how to actively apply it.
5. A 100-percent, satisfaction-guarantee is offered. Marketers know on average only 3 percent of consumers will return a product. Even when a customer is unhappy with a product it will likely remain unreturned because:
   a. Consumers lose the return information (or it is hard to find).
   b. Consumers do not try the solution within the guaranteed time frame and instead vow to "Do-it-Later."
   c. Consumers assume their approach is wrong versus assuming the product is not the right fit. Perhaps the next time they try it something will turn out differently.

Sooner or later, the hope-infused product ends up dusty and ignored. Eventually we go back in search of another piece of hope, and try again. The cycle repeats, the Change Addiction is born, and instead of questioning the products we question ourselves: *Why can't we do it?* Then we seek a solution for: *Why can't we change?* And the cycle lives on.

What if true change is simple? What if the key to momentum is within reach—right now? No additional purchase needed; no batteries required. "Oh come on," skeptics might say. "If the answer was so simple I would have done it already." If this describes you, stick with me a few more pages. What do you have to lose?

THE FIVE-MINUTE MOTIVATOR

Choose one of the top Life Areas needing attention from your Action Plan that you have access to right now. Maybe it is the pile of dishes to wash or unload from the dishwasher or a basket of laundry to fold. Perhaps it is exercise (try jumping jacks, walking in place, or stretching), paying bills, or fixing a healthy snack. Maybe cleaning off your desk, returning a call, or journaling are on your Do-It-Later list. Avoid overthinking your choice—give yourself thirty seconds to pick.

Using a timer is ideal. If you are at home, consider using your oven timer. If you do not have a timer, then use your watch or whatever clock is available. After you finish reading these instructions, wait for the next minute to be displayed or set your timer to five minutes. Then immediately begin your chosen action. If you want immediate, quick results, you will not find a quicker tool that can be applied to virtually any area of life.

Need a Timer?

Visit www.online-stopwatch.com for quick access to an online timer.

Please do not just read these words and vow to "Do-It-Later." We know how that path unfolds and it isn't one that will take you where you want to go. In five minutes, STOP! Then come join me at the next paragraph.

Congratulations! You just implemented the most powerful tool for change: ACTION. Through decisive and directed action you *can* travel down your desired path. You are five minutes further along than you were a paragraph ago.

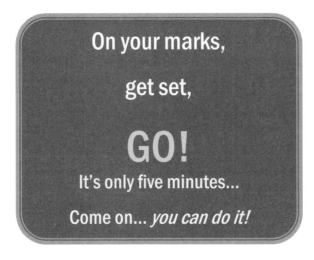

On your marks,

get set,

GO!

It's only five minutes...

Come on... *you can do it!*

THE POWER OF FIVE MINUTES

In a day and age in which "I don't have the time," tops the list of reasons for not achieving our desires, unleashing the true power of five minutes creates a dynamic shift in possibilities. What exactly can we accomplish in five minutes? Just about anything. Small steps can indeed create big results. Here's proof:

> ### *Chinese Bamboo Tree*
>
> *You take a little seed, plant it, water it, and fertilize it for a whole year, and nothing happens.*
>
> *The second year you water and fertilize it, and nothing happens.*
>
> *The third year you water and fertilize it, and nothing happens. How discouraging this becomes!*
>
> *The fourth year you water and fertilize it, and nothing happens. This is very frustrating.*
>
> *The fifth year you continue to water and fertilize the seed. Sometime during the fifth year, the Chinese bamboo tree sprouts and grows ninety feet in six days.*

I discovered the power of five minutes by accident. I once believed that change was complicated. For any change I wanted to implement, I would read, study, strategize, outline, and plan. My eye-opening moment came after one New Year Resolution. I vowed to run a marathon. I had run before, achieving a half marathon, and although I hadn't run in years, I felt that I could quickly get back in the habit. I downloaded a marathon training schedule. The first runs were three miles long. *No sweat*, I thought.

My assistant also made a resolution to begin exercising. She had long suffered from being overweight and found herself winded after a flight of stairs. She decided to use the onsite treadmill before lunch. "I am starting with two minutes," she shared. I rooted her on, excited she was taking a step forward. Meanwhile I silently cursed the outside weather; the rain would interfere with my first scheduled run. *No sweat*, I thought. *I'll just start tomorrow.*

As the cliché states, "someday isn't a day of the week." I never found this to be truer than three months into the New Year when my assistant and I shared our progress. "How is the running going?" she inquired.

"Not so well. I actually haven't even completed the first week of runs. It seems something always comes up, or the weather interferes, or my family needs me, or I am not feeling well. I am thinking I'll run a marathon near the end of the year so I can start my training schedule in a couple of months when things aren't so hectic. How about you?"

"I am up to three miles, six days a week," she replied.

"Wow! How did you do it?" I couldn't hide my amazement and admiration.

"I started at two minutes, and then worked up to three... and before I knew it, I was at three miles."

I thought of my marathon schedule and the two three-mile runs required in the first week that I had yet to complete. Meanwhile, my assistant had covered more miles than I had. While I had a history of running experience and was in shape, my assistant had something I lacked: my assistant had two minutes.

I realized while *some* changes do require strategizing, reading, studying, and planning, all change requires *action.* I started writing the original version of this book in five-minute increments. I began my independent promotion efforts in five-minute openings during days I was already working twelve hours. Now when someone asks me how long it took to get where I am today, I smile, think of my assistant, and then answer, "About five minutes."

TAKE A STEP FORWARD

Whenever you are stuck, frustrated, or thinking too much instead of taking action, stop and do five minutes of a task. Like me, I think you will be amazed at how little steps add up over time.

TOOLS, RESOURCES, AND REFERENCES

- ☑ View our online event calendar for free Marathon Sprints where we join together in our secure online chat room and encourage one another as we sprint our way to success.
- ☑ Near a computer? Use the free timer at www.online-stopwatch.com
- ☑ For additional support and accountability, check out the Action Jam Room. For eighteen hours a day, seven days a week, our moderated room provides a place for MTM Members to practice Five-Minute, Ten-Minute or Twenty-Minute Motivators with a group of cheerleaders and a trained Community Motivator to answer any questions.
- ☑ Use the site instant messaging system to set up one-on-one sprint times with other members.

toolbox step 10

Self-Sabotage and Self-Belief

"Courage does not always roar. Sometimes, it is the quiet voice at the end of the day saying, 'I will try again tomorrow.'"—*Mary Anne Radmacher*

Ask one hundred people to define self-esteem and you are likely to hear one hundred different answers. The dictionary offers this definition: a realistic respect for or favorable impression of oneself; self-respect.

I define self-esteem as: a sense of self-trust, self-respect, and self-kindness that allows us to move forward confidently with a realistic, positive outlook in order to live our best lives. This definition summarizes a belief in one's self, and a sense of inherent self-worth. Self-care is present, treating one's self as kindly and supportively as one would treat loved ones and friends.

You will notice the words "move forward confidently" in my definition. When we finally find the right track and begin following it, why does something seem to come along and pull us from it like a magnet? Sometimes this something is external—new demands, doubt from a person whose support we would like, or a stressful situation. Other times this something is internal—doubt, an internal voice discouraging us, a sudden inability to keep going even when we know we want to keep going. This something is created by a wavering self-belief which in turn manifests as self-sabotage.

This wavering self-belief often lurks in the shadows, dashing our hopes or impeding our plans. Other times it acts like a semi-truck careening right into us. How can we explain the paradox of being able to motivate and support children, friends, family, and colleagues to move forward, yet flounder with moving ourselves forward?

Children, friends, family — they are close to us. The table below shows some obvious and basic differences among someone who is close to us, acquaintances and enemies.

Friendship Table

Close Friend	Acquaintance	Enemy
Able to share our emotions and feeling and life experiences because a strong trust is present.	Able to share certain pieces of information selectively because a strong bond of trust is not present.	Not able to trust at all, likely has betrayed our trust or belittled our feelings.
Can count on a close friend to be there when we need them.	Not a strong enough kinship to rely on in times of need.	Would not consider leaning on for help as they have either let us fall, or we think they might.
A close friend encourages and supports us when we are going through the good and the bad.	An acquaintance may either support or discourage us in specific areas.	Would discourage us in times of good and bad.
We feel refreshed and renewed after spending time together.	We typically do not feel a strong renewal, but we don't feel drained either.	We typically would feel drained afterward.
A close friend is honest.	An acquaintance may say what we want them to say, scared of hurting our feelings.	An enemy is dishonest and typically speaks untruths.
Makes recommendations to help us improve our lives or grow a talent, dream or desire.	May throw out a suggestion or idea for improvement, but is rarely part of the support team for implementation.	Does not believe we can improve or if they do, they certainly wouldn't tell us.
Encourages a healthy perspective when we are caught in a negative spiral.	Does not know us well enough to offer too much feedback or recognize a negative spiral.	Moves out of our way so the negative spiral can continue.
When we are stressed they can help soothe us and understand our needs.	When we are stressed, some might lend a hand.	Does not understand or care about our personal needs or stress level.

This is just a quick and simple overview of the differences in these relationship categories. Looking at this basic table, what type of people would you like to have around you?

Below, I have modified the table just a bit. Think about how you currently treat yourself. In each row, check the entry that most closely matches how you typically treat *you*.

This revealing exercise demonstrates the tendency to value others much more than we do the self. Many women attempt to make positive changes again and again without reconciling the tendency to be their own worst enemy. Contentment, balance, esteem, stability, and consistency require a kindness and attentiveness to one's self.

Imagine the golden rule was, "Treat others as you treat yourself," instead of, "Treat others as you would like to be treated." Based on the checkmarks in the friendship table, how would that look in your life?

	Positive Self-Esteem (like a close friend) Column A	Average Self-Esteem (like an acquaintance) Column B	Negative Self-Esteem (like an enemy) Column C
1	☐ Able to respect emotions, feelings and life experiences because a strong self-trust is present.	☐ Able to respect certain emotions and feelings because self-trust is present in some areas.	☐ Typically belittle your feelings and emotions.
2	☐ When times get tough, you take care of your self.	☐ You occasionally stop and take care of your self during a tough time.	☐ You blame your self for tough times or think you should be able to "magically cope" and wonder, What's wrong with me?
3	☐ You know that the good and bad are parts of life and remain positive and perseverant.	☐ While you enjoy the good times, the bad times are definitely challenging.	☐ You feel you have had more than your fair share of the bad, and must be undeserving of the good.

	Positive Self-Esteem (like a close friend) Column A	Average Self-Esteem (like an acquaintance) Column B	Negative Self-Esteem (like an enemy) Column C
4	☐ Time in solitude is refreshing and renewing.	☐ Sometimes time alone is a good thing, other times it is extremely lonely.	☐ Time alone is not good — your mind conjures up many negative thoughts or worries excessively.
5	☐ You are honest with your self. You accept your strengths and your weaknesses without judgment.	☐ While you except parts of your self, you judge other parts.	☐ You tend to focus on your shortcomings and discount or cannot see your strengths as others do.
6	☐ You actively seek solutions to help improve your life, or grow a talent, dream or desire. You problem-solve to overcome obstacles and reach the desired destination.	☐ You occasionally try something new, but more often than not, you do not see it through to fruition.	☐ You rarely try something new because things rarely work out.
7	☐ You can audit your thinking and quickly correct negative thought patterns.	☐ You are able to recognize some negative thought patterns and correct them, but others continue.	☐ You are unable to separate our thinking from the self and pass judgment on your behavior.
8	☐ When you are stressed, you most often focus on what is needed to regain balance.	☐ Sometimes you can cope with stress, other times it gets the best of you.	☐ Stress creates additional doubt, anxiety or worry and you are unable to stop the stress spiral from growing.

How do we learn to treat ourselves as well as we do others? What does it look like? The model of friendship in the table can point the direction.

CREATING AN S.O.S. LIST
(S.O.S. = SAVE OUR SELVES!)

Look at your responses in each column. For each of the eight areas where you placed a checkmark in Column B or C, brainstorm one "theme" you could apply to change that area and write it down in your journal.

Examples: Row 6 offers this under the positive self-esteem column: *You actively seek solutions to help improve your life, or grow a talent, dream or desire. You problem-solve to overcome obstacles and reach the desired destination.*

If I had placed a checkmark in column B indicating I occasionally try something new, but more often than not, I do not see it through to fruition, a "theme" to move toward positive self-esteem might be to choose something I have started but have not completed and take a step forward in that area today.

If I had placed a checkmark in column C indicating I rarely try something new because things rarely work out, a theme to move closer to positive self-esteem might be: Try something new.

TAKE A STEP FORWARD

Work through each of the rows to where you marked a response in columns B or C and add to your S.O.S. List. When you're done, choose one "theme" to apply to your life this week. Add it to your Personal Power Deck or write it at the top of your Active Task List in your CAN. Each week revisit this list to select a new theme. After you have worked through the list, return to this Step and reassess your self-treatment using the table. Create a new S.O.S. List to work from based on your findings.

toolbox step 11

Avoiding Burnout and Overcommitment: "No" and the Personal Quota

"If I was in charge of the dictionary, I would change the definition of the word should to Should—A way of saying your heart is somewhere else."—*Brook Noel*

We experience burnout and overcommitment when we cannot set or maintain clear personal boundaries. We may find ourselves saying "yes" when we know we should say "no." Repeated over time, this pattern often results in the sacrificing of personal and family goals.

Why we say "yes" and when we need to say "no"	
We say "yes" because we want to please someone.	If we say "yes" with the main intention of pleasing someone, eventually we will have so many people to please we will let someone down and feel guilty. It is easier for people to hear "no" up front than to be let down later.
We think we have time that we do not have or it is a good cause.	When we fail to plan our time, our days, and our lives, we can overestimate our available time and take on so many commitments we quickly become stressed. Avoid making quick decisions and make sure you have the time available before saying "yes."

We have become an easy target and someone is so persistent we cannot say "no."	We can say "no," we have just set a habit of saying "yes." If it is someone we are close with the best option is honesty. Explain you are under too much pressure right now and are unable to take on additional commitments. Say, "I am sure you can understand and respect that," before the other person jumps in. If it is not someone we are close with, then we can simply say, "Due to other commitments, I have to pass right now."
We don't know how to say "no."	It is better to say "no" than to be indecisive and build expectations that you might say "yes." People often say, "Let me think about it," and then are unable to say "no" later. It is better to be up front and say "I am sorry, I just can't add another commitment right now," or "I am sorry, I cannot contribute at this time." You don't need to justify or give further reasons—everyone has the right to say "no," it may just take a little practice.
We are unsure if we can help or not.	It is always easier to change a "no" to a "yes" than the other way around.

RULES FOR SAYING "YES"

In our goal to help others or please people, we often say "yes" quickly without thinking through the time and effort a "yes" requires. If you find yourself in that predicament, try these guidelines before saying "yes" in the future:

- Think about any commitments for at least twenty-four hours prior to agreeing. Try something like, "That sounds really good—but I need to check my schedule before I can commit. I will call you tomorrow at X to let you know if I can help."
- If it is something you are interested in, make sure you understand exactly what is needed from you and the complete picture of your time commitment. If you want to help, but can't help in the requested way, propose another option or try something like, "I really would like to help

you, unfortunately my schedule doesn't have room for that type of commitment right now. However, I could _____."

- Help in areas that match your core values instead of trying to help at everything. Check your Snapshot. Does helping with this commitment contribute to one of the core areas in which you are seeking improvement? If not, remember that you will be using up time that could otherwise be spent in one of the areas that needs more attention.
- When you agree, clearly outline the level of your commitment: "Yes, I could help with that two hours per week."

Something to think about: when in the past have you said "yes" when "no" would have been more in alignment with upholding your values and staying on target with your goals? How can you use the information in this Step to avoid that trap in the future?

CREATING A PERSONAL QUOTA

I use a quota system for deciding how much time I have per week for carpooling, volunteering, etc. If I have extra time I say "yes"; if I don't I say "no." This allows me to retain balance without the guilt of saying "no."

TAKE A STEP FORWARD

To set your own personal quota, choose an amount of time that you feel comfortable devoting to outside activities. Make sure to consult your calendar so you choose a realistic amount of time. Avoid choosing an amount of time that will leave you stretched too thin.

Each week, when someone asks you to do something "outside the norm," check and see if you have any quota time available. If yes, make sure that this endeavor is in alignment with your priorities and aligns with how you want to spend your valuable time. If no, politely decline. If your quota time is five hours per week, and you reach that each and every week, be proud that you consistently gave five hours, instead of feeling bad when you have to say "no" because the commitment would exceed quota.

TOOLS, RESOURCES, AND REFERENCES
☒ Listen in online or download a free mp3 of my audio on Overcoming Burnout.

toolbox step 12

Your Personal Power Hour

A man who dares to waste one hour of life has not discovered the value of life." —*Charles Darwin*

In 2005 I was moving so quickly from task to task that to-dos seemed to pile up without any time to do them. Out of my frustration was born the Power Hour, and it transformed my days. The Power Hour stops incoming tasks and information for an hour in order to process what is already on my to-do list. The Power Hour can be applied to personal tasks, work tasks, or both. Here is how it works.

Depending on the demands in your life, choose one to five hours per week to stop incoming information and process what is already on your plate. Spread these hours among the week in thirty- or sixty-minute increments. During this time:
- Do not look at incoming email messages.
- Do not answer the phone.
- Close the door to the room you are in and put up a do-not-disturb sign (if you can).

During this hour, all communication should be OUTGOING. This is for you to focus on contacting, sending, completing, or moving a task forward. Use the Power Hour for "stragglers." Tackle the odds and ends and little to-dos that add up to big stressors. If you send emails during your Power Hour, work offline for the hour to avoid being sidetracked by new emails. If you make phone calls, let incoming calls roll over to voice mail so you can focus on outgoing calls. By turning off incoming communication, the Power Hour provides a focused environment.

Examples from my Power Hour List

- *reading/responding to emails*
- *returning phone calls*
- *making weekend plans*
- *phone calls to friends/family*
- *making appointments for yourself or family members*
- *calling in prescriptions*
- *paying a bill*
- *finding the file someone requested*
- *ordering something online*
- *making a grocery list*
- *sending a thank-you note*
- *setting up auto-pay for a bill*

TAKE A STEP FORWARD

Choose when and where you will hold your Power Hour time and block the space in your calendar. Glance through your CAN and star any items that are perfect candidates for Power Hour time. (You can choose items from the Active Task List, Short-Term Task List, or any of your CAN notes.) During your Power Hour work through the starred items in order, completing as many as you can.

At first, you may find your daily list exceeds one hour due to a "backlog" from not having previous Power Hours. That's okay. Incorporate this tool as a regular practice and watch how quickly your list whittles down! Once caught up, maintain the Power Hour practice to stay on top of life management. If you have extra time take the rest of the hour to read a book, page through a magazine, or just relax — you deserve it!

toolbox step 13

Have an Ugly Day

"Do something every day that you don't want to do; this is the golden rule for acquiring the habit of doing your duty without pain." —*Mark Twain*

Have you ever had one of those days or weeks (or months) in which everything on your plate was something you did not look forward to doing? Despite Three-Step Action Lists, Power Hours, and CANS…we are human. Eventually we will find a list of less than desirable to-dos in front of us.

As we move forward in the *Challenge* and our positive outlook grows, completing these undesirable to-dos can become especially challenging. We may fear undertaking a negative task that may interfere with our positive progress.

When I was developing this program in 2003, I remember going to bed, working through my Nightly Reflection routine (which you'll learn in Step 15), only to come face to face with the bleak reality that there was not one thing on my list I felt positive about or motivated to do. I had completed many tasks and the only things left were undesirable. Yet whether or not I wanted to do them, they had to be done.

Just before drifting off to sleep that Sunday night, I had an idea. I would make the upcoming week an "Ugly Week." Since I knew Monday contained three tasks I was dreading, I would find more dreaded tasks to fill the rest of the day. I would do the same thing for Tuesday and each day for the rest of the week. Every morning I would create a three-item "But I don't wanna…" list in place of a

Three-Step Action List. The more annoying the task, the higher it would move on my priority list.

Monday morning came and I arose, determined to have my "Ugly Day." I believe in always doing your best, and I was determined to have the ugliest day ever! When the mail came, I didn't look at the fun stuff—just the bills. As I went through the day, I chose the tasks that went against my grain. I worked through the backlog of unattractive to-dos.

My husband asked me what was wrong. "Nothing," I barked. "I am trying to perfect having a very ugly day." My daughter peeked in and teased, "Is that why you are wearing an ugly outfit?" I tried to suppress my smile. "That's not funny. I am going to go dust the television instead of watch it," I said.

By the end of the week, something interesting had happened. I had marked off so many undesirable tasks that I was in an incredibly good mood!

TAKE A STEP FORWARD

When facing a backlog of undesirable to-dos, have an Ugly Day. Too often, these tasks remain undone and drain energy needed for other tasks. Incorporating just one unattractive task into a day can weigh some people down for the entire day. A periodic Ugly Day allows us to really get into the role and clean up, while remaining positive the rest of the days. Schedule an Ugly Day once a month, or once a quarter—as often as you need to wipe out the gunk and create a fresh slate.

TOOLS, RESOURCES, AND REFERENCES
  ☒ Want to get really ugly? Join us online four times per year for official Ugly Day Challenges. The person who completes the Ugliest Day receives a prize!

toolbox step 14

Giving Up the Cape

"I find it interesting that the very cape I tried to use to fly became so heavy it kept me on the ground." —Brook Noel

One day I was racing around town, errand to errand, mission to mission. When I stopped at my house to grab a few papers, the phone rang. It was a dear friend from California, so I carved out ten minutes to tell him about the hectic pace I had been leading for the past twenty-four hours.

The night before had brought a full-on Wisconsin blizzard. During the blizzard I went out to shake the snow off my old rosebush so the branches would not crack under the weight. Midshake I heard a crackling sound. I looked up to see several large flaming sparks coming from a neighbor's tree. A wire, weighted down by snow, was blowing against a fork in the old oak.

Realizing this was probably a fire hazard, I called the fire department. The fire department asked me to call the electric company. I did, and the woman on the other end said there were emergencies left and right due to the storm and those needed to be tended to first.

"But what about my flaming tree?" I asked.

"Well, we can't get to it until we fix the power outages. Would you mind just keeping an eye on it?"

"I guess not," I replied before hanging up the phone.

I was a little confused as to why the flaming tree wasn't an emergency, but always a trooper, I set up my "tree stakeout" and made a makeshift bed near the window using a few sofa pillows. While watching this thirty-foot tree crackle and spark, it occurred to me that if the tree were to fall, it would go through our roof. Realizing this could be a disaster, I rushed upstairs to rescue my husband, Andy, and daughter, Samantha, who were both sleeping soundly.

I gave Andy a shove, then pushed him, and finally roused him. He stared at me through one half-opened eye. His expression told me he was more concerned with his sleep than with safety and was not interested in moving downstairs. Fortunately, after a little prodding, I persuaded him to join me in my tree stakeout. I rescued then-eight-month-old Samantha from her crib and took her downstairs with us.

I resumed lookout duty while Andy created a longer makeshift bed for himself. Determined not to lose sight of the tree, I tried to stay awake. Despite my best citizen watch attempt, I fell asleep. Samantha did too, tucked securely between my husband and me.

I awoke around two that morning and glanced out the window. The tree was still there. Andy was still there. Samantha, however, was not. I shook Andy's shoulder. "Where's Sammy?"

"I'm not sure," he replied, shaking himself awake.

We began our search. Samantha had just begun the rolling phase and had rolled through three rooms and was on her way, full speed, to the kitchen. Nestling her in my arms, I resumed my place in our living-room-camp.

Samantha woke up two very short hours later with a scream like that of an elephant seal. Knowing this was probably one of her chronic ear infections, I bounced into action with my cooing and cuddling routine. I began to count the hours until the clinic would open. There were four hours between now and the clinic, an antibiotic, Sammy's comfort, and my sanity.

After a sleepless, scream-filled four hours and a quick shoveling of the snow in the driveway, I ran Samantha to the clinic. There, my suspicion of an ear infection was confirmed. Then it was off to the pharmacy. Then it was back to the house. A phone message was waiting from the forestry service. They would be coming out to take a look at the tree and wanted to make sure I was home.

Then it was off to my computer desk where I balanced Samantha on one leg while finishing an advertising campaign with my one free hand. Of course, the campaign was due at the photographer's that day. To deliver the campaign, I would have to drive forty-five miles in blizzard conditions with a sick child, around the schedule of the forestry service.

In my rush to meet deadline, as I hurried out of the house I forgot the ad and had to double back. During the doubling back, my friend from California had called and asked simply, "How's your day going?" I rattled off the adventures with the tree, the forestry service, the clinic, and the campaign.

"It's always something," he said in a soft voice. Though I couldn't see him, I knew he was smiling.

"What do you mean?" I asked.

"Last week when I called it was training your cat, starting a new book, and accepting a new campaign. The week before that it was making homemade edible clay with Sammy, giving painting lessons, and starting a novel while rewallpapering the kitchen. Why are you doing so much?"

"Well," I paused. "I…um…"

"Yes?"

"I don't do that much," I said meekly.

"You're going to go with that?" he questioned again. I remained silent. Then my friend offered four words that were a gift: "Give up the cape."

Shortly after that day, I began to work on giving up my Superwoman cape. Instead of trying to accomplish everything and please everyone, I began to focus on what was important to me and my family. I accepted that I alone cannot do everything, nor will there be time for everything, so I need to do what *matters*. Instead of wearing a cape with "Have it all!" as its slogan, I opted for wings with the slogan of "Make Today Matter."

Discarding the cape is one of the best things I have ever done for myself. I find it interesting that the very cape I tried to use to fly became so heavy it kept me on the ground. Instead of living up to the "shoulds" and "woulds" that bound my life, I now live by the motto of "Make Today Matter." The cape is something we all need to outgrow in order *to* grow.

Participating in soccer, scrapbooking, cleaning, cooking, sewing, working, party organizing, PTA, and church choir does not make one person "better" than another person, who does only one or two activities. Media and marketing have painted a message that the more you have and the more you do the more successful and fulfilled you will become. Quite the opposite is true. The person engaged in many activities is more likely to become haggard, frustrated, or burnt out.

TAKE A STEP FORWARD

In what ways have you been trying to do more than is realistically possible while still staying sane? Begin shedding your cape by stripping back unrealistic expectations. In your journal, write down all of the responsibilities you have assumed and expectations you have for yourself or others have for you. Then pretend this list isn't your own, but that of a friend seeking more contentment, balance, and joy. What advice would you give her for leading a more balanced life? Write down the advice you would give her, then apply it to your own life.

toolbox step 15

NIGHTLY REFLECTION
An Evening Routine to Nourish the Soul and Transform Chaos to Centeredness

Finish each day and be done with it. You have done what you could. Some blunders and absurdities no doubt crept in; forget them as soon as you can. Tomorrow is a new day; you shall begin it well and serenely..."
—*Ralph Waldo Emerson*

In Step 3 we cemented the Good Morning routine. Before moving onto the Mini-Makeovers, we will appropriately wrap up the Toolbox with a Nightly Reflection. An effective evening routine allows us to recap, release stress, and give thanks for the day while also preparing for the day ahead. This Step is divided into two parts preparation and the actual routine that ties together the Steps in the Toolbox.

PART ONE: THE PREPARATION

From the original supply list, gather six nine-by-twelve white paper envelopes and the two expanding folders. Applying these directions is easiest if you first gather the supplies and then complete each component as you go along.

PAPER ENVELOPES

Use tape or a stapler to attach the printables to the envelopes as outlined below.

1. Create two Active Task Envelopes by attaching two separate Active Task List worksheets to two 9 x 12 paper envelopes.

At the top of one envelope, write the current week. At the top of the other, write the next week. (By placing relevant material into the second envelope during the nightly processing you create an "Active Task List on deck," to make transitioning to a new week quick and simple.

Remember to calculate the week by day and not date, just like the Active Task List in your CAN. In the example I shared my week always begins on a Monday and runs through Sunday. I do my weekly planning each Sunday (if needed, review Step 7 for a refresher on this concept).

2. Attach the Power Hour worksheet to a 9 x 12 envelope. Put today's date in the top blank.

3. Attach the Short-Term worksheet to a 9 x 12 envelope. Write the date it will be in sixty days at the top. For example, if today is July 1, then in sixty days it would be September 1, and the envelope would be labeled "Before September 1." If you are completing this on February 8, the envelope would be labeled "Before April 8."

4. Create two financial envelopes by attaching one copy of the Financial Record worksheet to two separate envelopes. Label one envelope with the current month, and the other envelope with the upcoming month. Example: If you are setting up these envelopes in January, then one envelope would be labeled January and the other would be labeled February.

5. Label one of the expanding envelopes "To Read." Label the other expanding envelopes "To File"

Note: If you do not have expanding envelopes, paper envelopes will work fine.

If you are using the worksheets from the workbook, MTM or shop, they are color coded. Here is a quick reference guide for the color sheets:
Pink = Active Tasks
Blue = Power-Hour
Purple = Short-Term
Green = Financial Record

Power Hour Items for _____

Due Date	Description	Contact Info	Notes	Done
				☐
				☐
				☐
				☐
				☐
				☐
				☐
				☐
				☐
				☐
				☐
				☐
				☐
				☐
				☐
				☐
				☐
				☐
				☐
				☐
				☐
				☐

		Short Term	
Due Date	Description	Notes	Moved to Active

☐
☐
☐
☐
☐
☐
☐
☐
☐
☐
☐
☐
☐
☐
☐
☐
☐
☐
☐
☐
☐

Print additional copies of this worksheet online at www.brooknoelstudio.com

Active Task Information for the Week of _____ 2008

Due Date	Description	Notes	Done
			☐
			☐
			☐
			☐
			☐
			☐
			☐
			☐
			☐

Monday
Tuesday
Wednesday
Thursday
Friday
Saturday
Sunday

Financial Records for _____

Due Date	Amount	Company Name	Date Paid	Check Number	Confirmation Number

Print additional copies of this worksheet online at www.brooknoelstudio.com

Set up your envelopes.

KEEPING IT TOGETHER

It is important to keep your Headquarters and the envelopes we just created together when not in use. Except on rare occasions, these will remain at home. I suggest storing them in an easily accessible place. I keep mine in a decorative basket so I can leave them out, yet they blend in as a decoration. I can easily take the basket of materials upstairs, into the living room or kitchen, or wherever I like. Upright file crates or paper holders also work well, as do tote bags.

Choose where you will keep all of your supplies. Make sure to either go get the holder now, or to do so before beginning the Toolbox.

PART TWO: THE ROUTINE

I complete my Nightly Reflection right after dinner. I find this is a good time because everyone is up and about anyway so I am not interrupting anything. My daughter does her homework after dinner as well. I consider the Nightly Reflection my homework, and complete the routine at the same time and at the same table. Whatever time you choose, maintain it *consistently* to ensure this becomes a regular routine.

SORT THROUGH THE CATCH-IT COLLECTIONS

Take the paper from the Catch-It Collectors in Step 4 and sort as outlined below:

Receipts: write down any purchases on the financial envelope. If the receipt is one you will keep, put the receipt in the envelope. Otherwise, shred it.

> *Tip: For business owners or those with tax-related receipts: if it is a receipt you will need at tax time, highlight or star the entry to make tax preparation easier. If you have many tax receipts or file separate business taxes, use separate finance envelopes for business.*
>
> *Tip: If you turn in expenses reports, have a separate envelope for expenses reports. Write down each item in the same way. This will help you make sure all receipts stay together and can be turned in on time and avoid losing "little receipts" that add up to large amounts over time.*

Bills: Record the due date and the bill information. Throw away any extra flyers, offers, or paper accompanying the bill. Place the bill and the return envelope in one of the two financial envelopes depending on the date it is due. (The financial envelopes are covered in detail in the Money Matters Mini-Makeover.)

> *Tip for online bankers: if you use online banking for recurring payments, it is a good idea to make a monthly finance sheet that includes these payments. Even if they are automatic payments, you will then have an accurate picture of current spending for each month on the front of the envelope.*

Magazines/Newsletters/Brochures/Stuff-in-the-Printer: Place anything you want to read in the To-Read Envelope. This envelope tends to get bulky quickly since we often want to read more than we realistically have time to read. Be selective and rip out articles of interest and then recycle the rest of the magazine.

Going forward, when you have an appointment or event where there may be extra waiting time, take the To-Read Envelope with you. Since I carry a large bag, I keep it with me daily to take advantage of unexpected breaks in the day. Because of my occupation, my To-Read Envelope is usually packed. Carrying it daily has allowed me to stay current with my reading.

Other people's paper: If you have paper that needs to go to another family member, put it in the Catch-It Collector to give back. If it needs to go to someone outside of your home, place it in the Active Task envelope so you remember to give it to them.

Process any paper that falls into the aforementioned categories.

SORT THE REST OF THE PAPER INTO ONE OF THE FOLLOWING ENVELOPES:

Active Task Envelope: If it is paper, you will need to reference this week or next, place it in one of the two envelopes. Write down a summary on the front along with the due date, unless it fits one of the following two categories:

Power Hour Items: Then place it in the Power Hour envelope. Write a summary on the front. Now that you have this envelope in play, use it to track your Power Hour Items. On the days you hold a Power Hour, use this envelope as your list and note-taking area.

Short-Term Envelope: If the paper does not meet the requirements of the Active Task Envelope or Power-Hour Envelope but needs to be addressed by the date on your Short-Term envelope, place it inside, noting the due date on the front. If it does not have an exact due date, write "Flex." It will be given a due date when we tackle weekly and monthly planning.

Process any paper that falls into the Active Task, Power Hour, or Short-Term envelopes

You have now created a system to track the major actions we take and log on a daily, weekly, or monthly basis in the Short-Term.

Any remaining paper belongs in the "To File" Envelope. Think of this envelope as a To File or Review envelope. Right now, in the short-term, the information is not relevant. Leaving this paper mixed in with current paper will dilute efficiency and focus. The other envelopes you have created are concerned with *current action*. Everything required for current action has a home since all current actions require you to either (1) act on it,, (2) give it to someone else, (3) read it, (4) pay it, or (5) track it.

Within the To-File/To-Review envelope, some of the items may need to eventually move to the Short-Term or To-Read Envelopes. However, if you have set this station up according to the directions, none of the To-File contents are relevant until after the date on your Short-Term Envelope. Review the To-File contents on a monthly basis and transfer items to your action envelopes as needed. File the remaining. If you fill the envelope prior to month's end, transfer the contents to a box to review at month's end. For detailed information on how to set up a filing system, consider my e-book, *Preventing Paper Piles and Overflowing Files: Creating an Effective Paper Management System*.

GROUPING TIME

My programs divide the paper, goals, actions, and tasks in our lives into three categories:

1. Active: relevant to the current calendar week
2. Short-Term: relevant to the next sixty days
3. Long-Term: relevant more than sixty days from now

I created this method to encourage focus and efficiency. I discovered much of our stress comes from trying to control, influence, or manage tasks in the future. By isolating current active items we can get more done with less stress.

Looking too far into the future is like driving by looking at a map instead of the road. While a map may be necessary, the point is to consult the map from time to time, and then return our eyes to the road. The Active group is the road, the Short-Term is like a regional map, and the Long-Term is a national map. Daily we focus on the road, weekly we consult the regional map, monthly we consult the big map.

The Active Group is comprised of the following items:

The Active Task Envelope

The Power Hour Envelope

The Catch-All Notebook

The To-Read Envelope

The Catch-It Collectors

The Active Group comprises the items we look at on a daily basis for effective planning and life management. All of the other envelopes are consulted on a weekly or monthly basis. For example, during the Weekly Review we would move items from the short-term list to the active list. **Again, we don't need to do this daily, because the information is not yet relevant. Instead, keep your focus on the active areas you can control.**

EVENING ROUTINE STEP BY STEP

STEP ONE: PROCESS THE CATCH-IT COLLECTORS
Processing the Catch-It Collectors is always the first step of the Nightly Reflection. **It is very important** to avoid being sidetracked by looking at what you have previously put in the envelopes. The worksheets you have applied to the envelopes are created as a "quick-reference" to avoid having to wade through the contents.

STEP TWO: TRANSFER THE ACTIVE TASK LIST IN THE CATCH-ALL NOTEBOOK
Leave about five lines of space in your Catch-All Notebook and then draw a line to begin the next day or turn to a fresh page. Write the date. Then leave a space for your Three-Step Action List. Do not create the Three-Step Action List yet.

If you have read my material before, you will not be surprised by what comes next. If you are new to my material this might strike you as a bit odd or as "busywork." It isn't. **I know that my efficiency and success are built on the foundation of three consistent practices:**

1. Keeping the Catch-All Notebook with me at all times and writing all my notes in it (Step 1 of the Toolbox)
2. The Three-Step Action List (Step 2 of the Toolbox)
3. Transferring the Active Task List (which you are about to learn)

Before passing judgment on the forthcoming technique as too much list writing, try it for thirty days consistently. I have challenged thousands of women to do so and to date every woman who has accepted that challenge has reported dramatically increased efficiency and improved results. Trust me—like you, I don't have time for busywork.

Transferring the Active Task List is the key to never forgetting anything, which also helps end procrastination and increase efficiency. Review your Active Task List in your Catch-All Notebook. Cross off or highlight any completed items. (I like to highlight items as it gives me a rewarding visual of what I have accomplished!) Take everything left on the Active Task List and transfer it to this fresh page below the space you left for the Three-Step Action List. Even if the list includes fifty items, rewrite it. Rewriting serves three primary purposes:

1. It ensures that you won't overlook anything.
2. It keeps all the "active items" fresh on your mind.
3. There are certain tasks that, for whatever reason, we don't like doing. These items tend to stay on a to-do list for a long, long time. We get used to just glancing over them and looking at the next item that we want to-do. When you rewrite "FERTILIZE THE LAWN" over and over and over and over and over, it will really begin to grate on your nerves. I guarantee that one day a little piece of you will wake up determined to cross off that item. Each time you rewrite a to-do item, you are planting an action-seed in your subconscious. One day that seed will bloom, and voilá—you can cross the item off your list. I know it sounds repetitive, but trust me— this practice can revolutionize your productivity and results.

Several times I have abandoned this practice and instead opted for a BlackBerry, Outlook task list, or other computerized option. While the electronic options made the process of list creation easier (and prettier) and I had less written-work, my efficiency plummeted. Since then I have learned quite a bit of neuroscience to explain why this was the case. Without going into a longwinded explanation, basically the mind is quite selective when viewing written words. The brain can avoid certain words altogether and often reads what it *thinks* is on the page, versus what is *actually* on the page.

> *By rewriting the Active Task List instead of glancing over the active actions we need to take, we reinforce them.*

Place a paper clip or binder clip on the current page to make it easy to find in your notebook.

STEP THREE: REVIEW THE ACTIVE TASK ENVELOPE

Review your Active Task envelope for any items you will need to handle tomorrow. Add these items to the list in your CAN.

STEP FOUR: DECIDE IF YOU WILL HOLD A POWER HOUR TOMORROW

Make a space for your Power-Hour Items if the next day you will hold a Power Hour or half-hour. If you have any undone items from your previous Power Hour, carry those over first. Check your Power Hour envelope for any items you will need. I keep a running list of all my Power-Hour tasks on the envelope. Then on Power-Hour days the envelope goes with me.

STEP FIVE: CREATE YOUR THREE-STEP ACTION LIST

With all of your active information reviewed and collected you are ready to create your Three-Step Action List. Add that in the space left blank just after the date.

STEP SIX: GIVING THANKS FOR THE DAY

Melody Beattie writes, "Gratitude turns denial into acceptance, chaos to order, confusion to clarity. It can turn a meal into a feast, a house into a home, a stranger into a friend. Gratitude makes sense of our past, brings peace for today, and creates a vision for tomorrow." Her words couldn't ring more true. It is through conscious gratitude that we realize the simple joys that make life rich and complete.

Sarah Ban Breathnach, in her best-selling book *Simple Abundance: A Daybook of Comfort and Joy,* advocates the use of a gratitude journal. She cites this as "a tool that could change the quality of your life beyond belief." I completely agree. The premise of the gratitude journal is to record five things that you are grateful for each day. Some days you might have to be creative to find five. Other days you might have ten or twenty! Value the little things. Value the person who sincerely smiled and asked how you were at the grocery store checkout. Value the soft touch of a child's hand on your shoulder or a favorite song heard on the radio.

Take a moment to think of things you are grateful for and record them in the space you left blank before creating your entry for tomorrow. Over time, notice how this deepens your appreciation for life and helps to maintain a positive outlook. This is also a good time to swap out your Personal Power Card, if you like, for a new inspiration.

STEP SEVEN: MAKE TODAY MATTER

Ask yourself, *Is there anything else I want to choose to do to make today matter?* Intentions and motivations are often strong in the morning but can evaporate with interruptions, distractions, and unexpected events. After 4 p.m., I have noticed, women tend to choose "I'll just do it tomorrow," versus valuing the time still left today. See if there is any little thing you would like to do yet today to move you forward in one of the areas your life needs attention.

STEP EIGHT: CLOSE THE SHOP

To echo the quote at the start of this Step: *"Finish each day and be done with it. You have done what you could."* Let go of expectations and undone tasks. As long as you are following the Toolbox Steps consistently, you can be sure **you have done what you could**. Now it is time to let go of to-dos and focus on the people around you, self-care, and enjoyment. Tomorrow will come soon enough. Try to keep your mind free from wandering to stressors and unfinished items. This will be challenging at first. As thoughts float by silently repeat, "Sorry, I'm closed. Please come back tomorrow. I reopen in the morning."

TAKE A STEP FORWARD

Practice the Nightly Reflection routine each evening until it becomes second nature.. Watch how this routine ensures your attitude and performance remain at their best — a necessary component of making each day matter in today's hectic world. In one week you will notice:

1. Less stress
2. More organization
3. Increased productivity
4. Less irritability and a more positive outlook
5. Increased contentment from directly choosing what to put into your day versus entering a new day unprepared.

Keep a copy of the Nightly Reflection Quick Reference with your envelopes. Use this as a quick-reference guide for completing the Nightly Reflection.

TOOLS, TIPS, AND RESOURCES
   ☑ Pre-printed colorful envelopes are available in the online shop.
   ☑ A printable evening routine quick-reference is available at the website.

Nightly Reflection Quick Reference

1. Process the Catch-It Collectors
2. Transfer the Active Task List in the Catch-All Notebook
3. Review the Active Task Envelope:
4. Decide if you will hold a Power Hour tomorrow
5. Create Your Three-Step Action List
6. Give thanks for the day
7. Make Today Matter
8. Close the shop

PART THREE
the mini-makeover collection

"Do what you can, with what you have, where you are."
—*Theodore Roosevelt*

The Mini-Makeover Collection in this book includes nine Mini-Makeovers, each with five Steps, which will help you increase satisfaction in a variety of life areas.

Before beginning the Mini-Makeover section it is important to take a second Snapshot for two reasons:

1. Implementing the Toolbox Steps can help align many Life Areas and create a different Snapshot.
2. Time passes, life changes, and a new Snapshot will reflect these changes.

A Snapshot, just like a photo, captures a period in time. Maybe finances were a stressor fifteen Steps back, but you have won the lottery since then. If so, my guess is that finances are not as high a priority as before, and you are more satisfied in this area.

We cannot manage what we cannot measure. Sometimes a program becomes ineffective because *the participant changes*. If a woman continues in a specific program without evaluating these changes, she will face frustration and may abandon the entire program.

The Snapshot provides a tool to continue measuring and managing progress. In the MTM Online program, after working through the Toolbox, members complete a new Snapshot each month. I encourage you to take a Snapshot monthly too. In the Appendix of this book you will find a quick reference sheet for each Life Area on the Snapshot and a list of Steps to revisit if that Life Area is a priority on your Action Plan.

Make sure to date each Snapshot and Action List and place behind the Snapshot tab in your Headquarters. These Snapshots become a revealing reflection of your journey. Over time you may also discover personal patterns. For example, one woman noticed how her main hat, spirituality, and time with children Life Areas continually "dipped" simultaneously.

Return to Part One and work through Getting Started Steps 2 and 3 to create a second Snapshot and Action Plan for change.

DESIGNING A MINI-MAKEOVER PATH TO MEET YOUR NEEDS

The second Snapshot and Action Plan will help navigate a Mini-Makeover path to address your prime concerns first. Locate the top area on your Action Plan in the list below. Begin with the Mini-Makeover that corresponds to this area. Once complete, move onto the next area on your Action Plan. Continue working in this fashion for a month. After one month, retake your Snapshot in order to keep actions and priorities in alignment. While you may not get to every area right away, you will get to the most needed areas, and the rest will be here when you need them.

Snapshot Area	1st Mini-Makeover	2nd Mini-Makeover	3rd Mini-Makeover
Relationship with significant other	Family matters		
Relationship with children	Family matters		
Relationship with friends and family	You've Gotta Have Friends	Family matters	
Self-time	Self, Sanity and Centeredness	Chaos and Clutter Clearing	
Attitude and out-look	Self, Sanity and Centeredness	The Worn-Out Woman	Here's to Your Health!
Money Management	Money Matters	Chaos and Clutter Clearing	Family Matters
Self-esteem	The Worn-Out Woman	Self, Sanity and Centeredness	Joy and Purpose-Filled Living
Household maintenance	Housework Helpers	Chaos and Clutter Clearing	Family Matters
Health	Here's to Your Health!		
Energy	The Worn-Out Woman	Here's to Your Health!	
Religion and spirituality	Joy and Purpose-Filled Living		
Main hat	Self, Sanity and Centeredness	The Worn-Out Woman	Joy and Purpose-Filled Living
Community	Joy and Purpose-Filled Living		
Meal planning	Housework Helpers		

Snapshot Area	1st Mini-Makeover	2nd Mini-Makeover	3rd Mini-Makeover
Information management *	Chaos and Clutter Clearing	Family Matters	Either Money Matters or Housework Helpers (depending on information to manage)
Time management *	Chaos and Clutter Clearing	Self, Sanity, and Centeredness	Either Money Matters or Housework Helpers (depending on what area needs improved time management)

* Information management and time management are covered mostly within the Steps learned in the Toolbox. When these Steps are applied consistently they will alleviate time and information overload in all life areas. If you are seeking in-depth monthly and quarterly planning, consider joining the MTM Online where each month we complete a Snapshot, Action Plan, and monthly planning checklist.

MINI MAKEOVER: CHAOS AND CLUTTER CLEARING

Have you ever felt like if you had a little room to breathe and space to focus, you could live a richer life? Is daily joy lost in the hustle and bustle? The Steps in this Mini-Makeover will help you replace chaos, clutter, and complications with a calmer, simpler life.

MINI-MAKEOVER: SELF, SANITY, AND CENTEREDNESS

A person cannot be pulled in too many directions for too long or self and sanity will suffer. If you feel stretched to the limit, this Mini-Makeover can help you reclaim sanity and centeredness.

The five Steps will guide you through reconciling your emotional energy account and implementing basic sanity-savers.

MINI-MAKEOVER: MONEY MATTERS

Almost unanimously, women rate finances as a top stressor. When finances are tight, attitude and outlook are affected. But no matter where you are financially, there are steps that can put you on the road to financial freedom. This Mini-Makeover will help you change your thinking about money, manage day-to-day spending, and overcome impulse spending once and for all.

MINI-MAKEOVER: FAMILY MATTERS

In today's hectic world managing day-to-day family matters can seem more difficult than putting a man on Mars. This Mini-Makeover shares strategies for handling common errands, using chore and reward systems with kids (or for you!), and keeping a well-bonded family unit.

MINI-MAKEOVER: YOU'VE GOTTA HAVE FRIENDS: FOSTERING A POSITIVE SUPPORT NETWORK

One of the greatest influences to anyone's quality of life is the people around them. It is impossible to achieve balance without balancing relationships. From friendships to colleagues to relatives, this Mini-Makeover takes you step-by-step through "organizing the people in your life." You'll learn who you need to have on your team, how to handle negative people, and how the people in your life affect you.

MINI-MAKEOVER: JOY AND PURPOSE-FILLED LIVING

Have you ever felt there must be "something more" but found yourself unable to identify what it is? Have you ever felt your life is a series of to-dos but that you aren't really living? These feelings are often caused by a disconnection between actions and values. This

Mini-Makeover will help you rediscover passion, values, purpose, and joy in your life.

MINI-MAKEOVER: THE WORN-OUT WOMAN

Feel like you are stuck in a rut or worn out? Perhaps all you need is an "Attitude Makeover." In this Mini-Makeover you'll learn easy-to-implement strategies and self-coaching strategies to actively take control of your thoughts and make changes that will help you achieve greater happiness, joy, and contentment.

MINI-MAKEOVER: HERE'S TO YOUR HEALTH!

Have you tried more than one diet or exercise regimen? More than ten? Have you been focusing on what you eat (counting grams, calories, or points) instead of on behavioral changes that last a lifetime? This Mini-Makeover explores food, fitness, and ideas you can implement to easily begin living a healthier life today.

MINI-MAKEOVER: HOUSEWORK HELPERS

In this Mini-Makeover you will learn how to formulate a game plan to manage household maintenance: we'll create a Master Task List, learn a Simple Six-Box Sort and Stow Solution, recreate the dinner hour with Rush-Hour™ meal plans, and implement a daily sprint system to keep it all under control.

Reminder: Continue using the same pacing guidelines throughout the Mini-Makeover section.

1. Complete each Step thoroughly before moving onto the next.
2. Implement a maximum of five Steps each week.
3. Do not implement more than one new Step on any given day.

Looking for more Mini-Makeovers? You can download additional Minis from the shop at www.brooknoelstudio.com

mini-makeover

Chaos and Clutter Clearing

"Life is really simple, but we insist on making it complicated." —*Confucius*

Have you ever felt that if you had a little room to breathe and space to focus, you could live a richer life? Is daily joy lost in the hustle and bustle of life? The Steps in this Mini-Makeover will help you replace chaos, clutter, and complications with a calmer, simpler life.

Step 1: Chaotic Confessions: Confronting the Complication Addiction

Step 2: The True Cost of Clutter

Step 3: Unraveling the Complicated Life

Step 4: Create a Space

Step 5: Junk Mail, Anyone?

chaos and clutter step 1

CHAOTIC CONFESSIONS
Confronting the
Complication Addiction

"There is nothing so useless as doing efficiently that which should not be done at all."—*Peter Drucker*

I confess, I am a complicated person. Some people believe we are born simple, with basic needs of food, love, shelter. Not me—I was born complicated. I came into the world in forty-five minutes, allergic to practically everything. I could not drink milk or be near rubber or plastic, thus requiring cloth diapers. (Just ask my mother— she will verify how unsimple that was.) At birth I had strabismus, an eye condition that led to three surgeries by the age of three and several more surgeries before the age of eighteen. When I was four I asked my mother to explain the meaning and purpose of life. My mother would testify that I have had an ever-racing, spinning and complicated mind…until recently.

When the simplicity movement burst on the scene a decade or so ago, I'll be honest—I thought it was for people who couldn't keep up with life. I didn't realize then, as I do now, that simplicity is for people who want to keep up with *their* life and not the life sold to millions on television and within glossy books. I, like many of us, had bought into the hype that the more I had, the more I did, the more I squeezed into a day—the richer my life would be. The thought of scaling back made my stomach churn. Only recently did I discover complications and chaos do create excitement and momentum, but rarely do they create any lasting joy, happiness, contentment, or the peace we so desperately crave. Constantly moving forward, we are unable to enjoy the now. A person cannot be present in the now if she is on her way to the next thing, the next chase, the next task, the next goal.

As I honestly assessed my life, I could see the complicated cycles repeating more quickly than a Mountain Dew-consuming hamster on a wheel. People who know me well would tell you my life has always been chaotic and cycling. And until recently, I would tell you that many of the chaotic events were random, completely outside of my control.

We would both be right—to a point. Because I am involved in so many ambitious activities, I do tend to attract a variety of circumstances outside the norm. Yet who is responsible for these many ambitious activities? Who made the choice to engage or disengage? I did. I chose the complicated life, always wanting to be at the front of the pack, never wanting to miss a thing, constantly curious about what lies around the next corner.

It took many years for me to admit I was the primary creator and controller of chaos. I began to see a pattern in which time finally opened in my schedule, only to be overfilled within an hour. I saw how again and again I would run to help others, even though it left me overextended. I saw the tendency to be the helper, but to never ask for help. Most of all, I realized I created this chaos because I was trying to "be something," to matter. I was trying to be *everything*.

When I first heard the word "simplicity," I imagined living in a teepee and turning off electricity. I saw myself in a Laura Ingalls Wilder dress carrying a bucket of water for hand-washing clothes. Eventually I realized a simplicity movement could be extreme, but it needn't be so. I prefer to think of it as uncomplicated. I began a personal "Uncomplicate Routine" in my life.

For me, an Uncomplicate Routine involved the decision to run my own life. The time had come to step off the treadmill into a day in which I am living deliberately—making conscious decisions to foster joy.

The Uncomplicated Life involves trading "busyness" for meaning, confusion for clarity, expectations for personal peace. Uncomplicating your life means spending less time chasing and more time enjoying; spending less time acquiring and more time experiencing; spending less time managing life and more time living.

Here's the catch, of course — getting off the treadmill is not easy. We have to combat the many messages we see and hear every day. Instead of buying-in to our commercial culture, we strive to opt-out and forge our own path. The reward for those who accept the challenge is great. Instead of living a life on auto-pilot, we design a life through clear decisions in alignment with joy and values.

TAKE A STEP FORWARD

Look at each Life Area in your second Snapshot. Have you chosen to overschedule, overcommit or otherwise create complications or chaos? For any Life Area in which the answer is yes, write down the ways you have created complications in your journal. Make sure to describe the specifics of each situation. (Observing the ways you most often complicate your life helps create an awareness to stop repeating the chaos going forward.)

Star the three items on this list currently causing the most chaos. For each item write down a clear action you can take to simplify and reduce stress. Implement at least one of these three actions before moving onto the next Step. Add the other two to the Active or Short-Term Action List in your CAN.

chaos and clutter step 2

THE TRUE COST OF CLUTTER
How "Stuff" Robs Time,
Energy, and Wallets

"Unnecessary possessions are unnecessary burdens. If you have them, you have to take care of them! There is great freedom in simplicity of living. It is those who have enough but not too much who are the happiest." —*Peace Pilgrim*

Clutter, whether emotional or physical, is the number one robber of simplicity. Clutter takes up free thought and free space in which energy could otherwise roam. Try this simple experiment to see how clutter affects you.

Walk into the most cluttered area of your home. Start a timer for ten minutes and stand in the room. Do not pick up anything or begin rearranging or decluttering. Just stand in the clutter and absorb it, imagining you will later need to recount as many objects within the room as possible.

After the ten minutes have passed, move to the least cluttered area of your home. If everything is cluttered, go outside. Stand in this space for ten minutes. Once again don't "do anything" —just "be." What difference did you feel? (Note: to read this exercise on paper will not offer the same benefit as doing it and feeling the difference between space and clutter.)

When women do this exercise with me, they often respond with:

- "I literally felt like in one area I was choking and in the other area I could breathe."
- "I felt hopeless and lost amongst the piles. There was clarity when I was outside."

- "I felt a lot happier in open space...instead of mixed amongst all the things I thought I needed to be happy!"

Truth be told, it doesn't take much to make a person happy. Most of happiness's components cannot be found in store aisles or catalog pages. Not only do we not find happiness within the stuff, we pay a high price for clutter.

TAKE A STEP FORWARD

In your journal, create a page with three columns labeled Item, Money, and Time. Go back to your cluttered area, pick up an item and ask: "If right this moment I could trade this item back for either the money I spent, the time I spent choosing and maintaining it, or both, would I?"

If you answer "no," move on to the next item. If the answer is yes, write down the name of the object in the item column. Next record how much this item has cost you. Lastly record how much time you have spent on the item (including purchasing, caring for, dusting, maintaining, learning how to use, thinking about, etc.) Just estimate—mark down whether it's a little, medium, or a lot of time. Continue working through each object in this manner.

After completing the clutter space or filling one page (whichever comes first) total the columns. This is the true cost of clutter. This is the time and money you have given to "stuff" that has not added value to your life. Let this awareness exercise be an inspiration to think twice about buying "stuff" in the future.

TOOLS, RESOURCES, AND REFERENCES
    ☑ Additional printable copies of the True Cost of Clutter Worksheet are available online.

chaos and clutter step 3

Unraveling the Complicated Life

"The ability to simplify means to eliminate the unnecessary so that the necessary may speak."—*Hans Hofmann*

I have always been somewhat annoyed by my coffeemaker. Actually, I don't have anything personal against my current device, but a frustration with coffeemakers in general. My past seven coffeemakers have all worn out within eighteen months, and each had its own unique quirk. With the majority, no matter what carafe, pot, pitcher, funnel, or liquid tool I used to fill the system, I would end up with water all over the counter.

I also like to grind my beans fresh. Again, no matter my method, my counters would be littered with coffee grounds as I sought a fresh brew; sometimes the grounds even ended up in my cup.

On a completely separate note, I also have a scissor dilemma. No matter how many pairs I buy, as soon as I need a pair they have disappeared. I won't even go into my challenges of solo socks and how these perfectly happy couples emerge from the dryer solo.

What do my coffeemaker, socks, and scissors have in common? All three are tolerances. While not earth-shattering problems, each is a complication in the day; a complication I accept instead of solve. I do not fall into a depression when encountering these obstacles, but they do frustrate me. Instead of providing peace, each time I see the seeping water I shake my head and reach for a rag.

Each of us has our own tolerances. Tolerances make up the list we "will get to" someday when there is time. Yet if we face a certain tolerance often, then today is the day to think about removing this stressor and simplicity stealer from your life.

Here are a few examples of tolerances:

- No garbage can in the laundry room for the lint
- Junk mail
- No napkins/clean up supplies/garbage bag in the car
- Piles of twisted cords that we don't know what are for
- Running out of AA batteries
- Running out of essential supplies such as milk
- Socks that don't match
- Too many plastic bags
- Pieces and parts to "something"
- Items to give away that haven't been
- Missing scissors, tape, and staplers
- Tangled Christmas lights
- Clothes that don't fit or look good
- Wobbly chairs and tables
- Expired warranties
- Too many clothes hangers
- Junk drawers
- Drawers which don't close
- Storage containers without lids
- Expired coupons
- Cosmetic products that are outdated, or don't match, or don't work
- Stacks of old magazines we don't read

This is just a small list of the many things that complicate our lives today. Solving just one tolerance once and for all rejuvenates and simplifies our world.

TAKE A STEP FORWARD

Tolerances take up a lot of time and energy, but resolving them is often a quick process. Generate your own list of life tolerances in your journal. Choose five items from this list and brainstorm ways to resolve them. Add one tolerance brainstorm to your Active Task List and the other four to your Short-Term Action List.

TOOLS, RESOURCES, AND REFERENCES

☒ Share your "tolerances" online and make a commitment to remove them. Learn what other members are tackling and how.

chaos and clutter step 4

Create a Space

"Have nothing in your houses that you do not know to be useful or believe to be beautiful." —*William Morris*

Comedian George Carlin does a great routine on clutter. "A house is just a pile of stuff with a cover on it. Everybody's got a little place for their stuff. This is my stuff, that's your stuff, that'll be his stuff over there. If you didn't have so much stuff, you wouldn't need a house. You could just walk around all the time. That's what your house is, a place to keep your stuff while you go out and get…more stuff!" Many of us can relate all too well to this dialogue.

In our society, much emphasis has been placed on acquisition. We work to acquire this and that and constantly fill our lives with more and more stuff. Of course the irony is that one of life's biggest joys is simplicity itself.

If you have an issue of *Architectural Digest* or any other home magazine, glance through its pages. Find a spacious room or house. Notice how inviting space becomes. I think this kind of wide openness is attractive to most of us since our lives are more packed than ever. Whether our days are filled with duties to do or items to maintain, they have become overwhelmingly complex. Simplicity offers a space and freedom to escape from a crammed lifestyle.

GUIDELINES FOR CUTTING CLUTTER

Choose a room (or an area within a room) to implement clutter-free living. Start with an area where you often sit (or would sit if there was room). Each day, spend ten or twenty minutes or more simplifying the contents. Decide what items you are not willing to give any more time or energy. Only you can put your foot down and stop giving your time and energy over to clutter. Remove items you refuse to let complicate your life anymore and make a plan to get them out of your house within a week. You can sell them on eBay. You can donate them to a school, library, or church. You can throw them in a dumpster. But let them go. Don't move them into another area of your home—let them go.

When you find yourself getting nervous about letting go of an item, or feeling tempted to save it for a rainy day, ask: *how has this contributed to my happiness? Does this item truly bring me more happiness (or happiness to a member of my family)?* If the answer is "no," then get rid of it. Items are not neutral. They either enhance our lives or detract, by taking up energy and space.

If you are a serious packrat and are terrified of letting go, then box like items together. Seal the boxes well and put them somewhere else, the basement, the attic, anywhere except in your clutter-free zone. Write a date six months from now on the box. Label the box so you know what is inside. In six months, visit your stash of boxes. Odds are you will have found the joy in simplicity and be able to part with at least some of these stashes.

TAKE A STEP FORWARD

This simple exercise might help you change your thinking about "what to keep" and "what to toss," and what brings value and richness to your life. Begin taking action by decluttering the room (or area within a room) of your choice. Spend ten to twenty minutes a day decluttering until you are satisfied with the result.

TOOLS, RESOURCES, AND REFERENCES
   ☒ Take advantage of the online Action Jam room for motivation while completing ten or twenty minute sprints.

chaos and clutter step 5

Junk Mail, Anyone?

"Our life is frittered away by detail...Simplify, simplify." —*Henry David Thoreau*

Glance through a paper pile and you will likely find that much of the paper came into your life without your involvement. Welcome to the world of junk mail. Junk mail is not only infiltrating our snail mailboxes, but our telephones and email inboxes as well.

It is estimated that in the United States alone, four million tons of junk mail goes out each year—*and almost half of it is never opened!* Besides being a temptation and time-waster, the environmental impacts are enormous. There are many reasons to reduce junk mail. Here are a few:

- Become more environmentally friendly
- Save money by less temptation
- Reduce your paper clutter
- Save time by not dealing with it
- Increase contentment by not staring at things you don't have

These mailers are typically packaged in tantalizing envelopes, featuring key phrases that have been proven to encourage paper retention. Here are some of the most commonly used marketing phrases and an interpretation guide for what they *really* mean. (This is a tongue-in-cheek guide—obviously some offers do make sense. Also, I am not claiming to be immune to these temptations. My succumbing to these temptations time and time again is what has made me a pro in my tongue-in-cheek interpretations!)

Act soon! Limited Time Offer! This offer expires in 14 days! (Interpretation: If you don't act soon, we will send you a different offer that you might act on soon.)

This will be your last catalog! (Interpretation: Until we print the next one.)

No interest for 12 months! Pay nothing now! (Interpretation: We know you are an optimist and will believe you will have money available in twelve months that is not available now.)

Receive $1,000,000 in bonuses by spending just $9.99: (Interpretation : We need to use up all the items we couldn't sell in failed promo attempts, so we have set the value higher and will send them to you.)

Lifetime Guarantee! (Interpretation: If you remember to return the little registration card.)

You are pre-approved! (Interpretation: Our approval process has 104 levels and like everyone else, you have qualified for the first approval level—which is having a valid mailing address so we can reach you.)

STOP THE MADNESS!

Completing the action steps outlined below will take twenty to thirty minutes, but this is nothing compared to the time it takes to process junk mail and maintain, cancel, return, or regret a purchase. These strategies should drastically reduce incoming junk for three to five years, at which time you will likely have to repeat the process.

The Big One—Bulk Mail: The Direct Marketing Association can drastically help reduce your junk mail through a few simple steps. They estimate that using their MPS (mail preference service) will stop 75 percent of national mailing. Each month they process over fifty thousand requests and your information is kept on file for five years. It can take up to six months for your request to be fully processed. You can also opt-out online, but they charge one dollar. To avoid a charge, simply fill out the form, print a copy, and follow the mailing instructions. https://www.dmaconsumers.org/cgi/offmailing.

Specify: If you donate money, order a product or service, order something via phone, order something online, or fill out a contest form, make sure to say or write: "Please do not sell, share, or rent my name or address." This will help with most companies, but not all.

First class mail: Cross out the address and bar code, circle the first class postage and write "refused: return to sender." Drop in any mail box and it will be returned. Most companies will then remove you from the list, versus spending additional marketing monies on mail that won't be opened.

Credit offers: The major credit agencies sell information, and this is a major source of junk. To stop this mail, gather your address, any other addresses used in the past two years, and your social security number. Call 1–888–5 OPT OUT (or 1–888–567–8688) twenty-four hours a day, and you will be opted out of all the agencies' mailers — Equifax, Trans Union, Experian and Innovis, a large provider of pre-approved offers.

Catalogs: Call the 800 number with the mailing label handy and ask to be removed.

America Online: Thousands of free trial disks? To opt-out of this list, call 1–800–605–4297 (twenty-four hours a day).

Publisher's Clearinghouse Sweepstakes: Contact customer service at 1–800–645–9242 (8:30 a.m. to 8:30 p.m. EST).

Local business & supermarket fliers: These are generally provided by several groups:
- ADVO: Call 1–860–285–6100 to get off the list.
- Val Pak: Visit the Internet site and fill out the easy form, but don't give them your email address. http://www.coxtarget.com/mailsuppression/s/Display MailSuppressionForm
- Carol Wright: Call 1–800–67-TARGET to get off the list.

WHILE WE'RE AT IT

While we're at it, we might as well reduce the incoming calls that interrupt your time to deal with paper. Federal law prohibits telemarketers from "initiating an outbound telephone call to a person when that person previously has stated that he or she does not wish to receive an outbound telephone call made by or on behalf of the seller whose goods or services are being offered." You may simply interrupt the telemarketer and say "**Please permanently remove me from your calling list.**" If the same people call back, they are violating the law. If you get a lot of telemarketing calls, keep a notebook by your phone and write down the company, time, date and name of the person you spoke with. Ask them for their company name, supervisor name, and phone number. If you wish to quote federal law to the telemarketer, you can find it online by searching for Federal Trade Commission: Telemarketing Sales Rule.

I remember a court case long ago in which a gentleman had been repeatedly called by a major credit card company after stating not to be contacted again. He took his case to court and the company was fined and he was awarded damages!

Just as the Direct Marketing Association offers a service to reduce junk mail, they can help with unwanted calls as well. Visit https://www.dmaconsumers.org/cgi/offphone to learn more.

Do not call registry: Visit the Do not call registry at https://www.donotcall.gov/default.aspx. You can be added to the registry at this government site by completing an online form. It takes about thirty-one days to begin seeing results. If you receive calls after that date, make sure to file a complaint at this same link.

TAKE A STEP FORWARD

Spend a Power Hour contacting these companies to remove your name and reduce the junk mail infiltrating your life.

TOOLS, RESOURCES, AND REFERENCES
    ☑ Visit the online resources for clickable links to remove your name and information from these lists.

mini-makeover

Self, Sanity, and Centeredness

"Trust yourself. You know more than you think you do."—*Benjamin Spock*

A person cannot be pulled in too many directions for too long or self and sanity will suffer. If you feel stretched to the limit, this Mini-Makeover can help you reclaim sanity and centeredness. The five Steps will guide you through reconciling your emotional energy account and implementing basic sanity-savers.

Step 1: Is Your Glass Half-Full or Half-Empty?

Step 2: Defining Decisions

Step 3: Reconciling Your Emotional Energy Account

Step 4: Operation Handbag

Step 5: Girls' Night Out

self and sanity step 1

Is Your Glass Half-Full or Half-Empty?

"The kindest thing you can do for the people you care about is to become a happy, joyous person."—*Brian Tracy*

While you might feel your number-one commitment is to your family, a passion, a vision, or another area, we all share the same number-one commitment and that is a commitment to self-care, kindness, and nurturing.

Don't begin reading more quickly or skipping this section altogether while thinking, "Yeah, right. Where would I find time for that?" I used to think that way, and my inefficiency showed it. The more I fought this universal truth, the more difficult my life was to manage.

Finding time for yourself isn't an option. We need to make the time.

Women are nurturers by nature. This is a wonderful and needed quality, but it has a dangerous downside. When we are too busy caring for others, we put self-care at the bottom of the list. While this may seem "admirable" or "noble," we aren't doing anyone any favors, especially those we are trying to care for. No matter how "strong" you believe yourself to be, or how independent, or how "different" than other women—you need to rejuvenate. Some women only take time to rejuvenate when they find themselves down, in a funk, or worn-out. By practicing self-care regularly, we can avoid many emotional lows.

Think of your life as a pitcher of caring. Each time you care and nurture, you pour some of this kindness onto others. If you refill it once a month, you will have to ration small portions to everyone or you will run out early in the month. If you refill it once a week, you can nurture a bit more, but will still have to use caution to have enough to go around. The only way to fill this pitcher is by recharging. When recharging is done daily, we feed our own souls, and fill the pitcher to care for others in the process. In addition to affecting those we care for, the fullness of this pitcher affects everything in our life from hobbies to work to home.

You are not a bottomless supply house of caring and energy. You can only give what you have. Would you expect your car to drive nonstop without refueling and maintenance? Of course not. Are you expecting yourself to run nonstop without refueling and maintenance? If you were a car, when was the last time you stopped for gas, had your oil changed, had your windows wiped clean? If you were a car, would you be worn out or rusted due to poor maintenance?

Very few people I know would buy a new car and run it into the ground without maintenance. Very few people could afford to do that. What is more valuable, your life or a new car? What gets better care—your life or your car?

TAKE A STEP FORWARD

Each day schedule at least twenty minutes, preferably thirty, to focus on "you." Many people wonder: what should I do with these thirty minutes? The answer: whatever you want. You don't need to decide today. When the scheduled time arrives, ask yourself: *What would refuel me today?* Some days it might be a walk. Other days it may be a coffee or a trip to a card shop. Some days you may want to nap or just read a book. There isn't a "proper" activity. The only guideline is that this twenty- to thirty-minute period is reserved for you and you alone. All your energy and attention is undivided and aimed at yourself versus others.

Refueling Resources

Consider adding rejuvenating activities that can be completed in twenty or thirty minutes to your Personal Power Deck. Group these cards together and pick one at random for a refueling idea.

These rejuvenation periods need to be a routine commitment. Each week, mark this time off in your calendar before adding other items. I cannot emphasize this enough, so let me say it one more time: **If you choose not to do this, please do not expect any major changes in your life to last.** While you may experience a flash of energy, ultimately you will be the car sitting on the side of the road waiting for a tow.

TOOLS, RESOURCES, AND REFERENCES

☒   Share or print refueling Personal Power Cards online.

self and sanity step 2

Defining Decisions

"Decisions, particularly important ones, have always made me sleepy, perhaps because I know that I will have to make them by instinct, and thinking things out is only what other people tell me I should do"—*Lillian Hellman*

In the midst of managing the home, preparing meals, working, appointments, obligations, and meeting commitments, decisions are often made quickly, with little time to think through repercussions. When life is overflowing, our tendency is to do the obvious (or easiest) instead of doing what is needed. Seemingly inconsequential decisions can create serious balance deficits that lead to feelings of anxiousness and stress.

Learning to be aware during the moment of decision is an important skill for regaining sanity and a more centered life. Every decision we make (or don't make) leads us in a direction. It either leads us toward the life we desire or away from it. *Our life is a reflection of the decisions we make.*

Below is a table of seemingly minor decisions a person might encounter in a day. At first glance the list looks trivial, but the impact column shows how each decision clearly influences a person's life quality.

When making a decision, double-check your choice by considering this: *what positive or negative impact will my decision have?* Sanity and centeredness are regained through handling current chaos effectively and actively preventing future stressors. Weighing

Seemingly Minor Decision	Impact
Should I stay up two extra hours to "play" on my computer or watch that television show?	Potential sleep shortage which will impair ability to focus and make clear decisions the following day. May also impair attitude toward others.
Should I let my child have the little $3 item they want to add to the grocery cart?	Might set a precedent and poor boundary for future shopping experiences; $3 on each grocery trip, added up for a child's lifetime, could pay 1/3 of college expenses if put in savings.
Should I subscribe to this magazine because it is 80 percent off the newsstand price?	Adds to perceived "things-to-do" since purchasing it means you should read it. Adds to clutter. Depending on magazine, might promote consumer culture.
Colleague comes in unannounced and wants to "chat" for ten minutes.	Depending on workload, this could leave you more stressed or make you late in getting home and spending time with family. Might also set a precedent for colleague and ten minutes compounded over time equals a lot of stress—and at least a day off!

decisions in the moment is the essential Step to minimizing future stress.

TAKE A STEP FORWARD

Action Step 1: For seventy-two hours, observe all of the decisions you need to make. Before deciding, reflect on the impact of your decision. Watch how your responses differ by maintaining awareness in the moment of decision.

Action Step 2: Make a conscious decision with regard to technology. Choose one or more of the following ideas to implement for at least one week. At the end of the week, evaluate how this conscious decision has helped to uncomplicate your life.

☐ Instead of mindlessly watching television, circle the shows you want to watch in the newspaper, TV guide, or by accessing your listings online. Set a limit of five hours. Do not watch anything not on your list.

☐ Turn off the television in your home for one week. Visit www.turnofftv.org for support and ideas.

☐ During the dinner hour, turn the ringer off on all phones.

☐ For the majority of a day turn the clocks in your home around (or cover digital clocks with a piece of paper). Live in the moment, instead of by the clock.

☐ Check email only once or twice per day. Limit your Internet and email time to one hour per day, thirty minutes in the morning and thirty minutes at the end of the day. Exit your email or Internet program outside of these times.

☐ For one week only, use your cell phone when outside of your home. Turn it off when entering the home.

☐ Screen your calls instead of being a slave to your phone. If it is important, a message will be left and you can pick up or return the call.

self and sanity step 3

Reconciling Your Emotional Energy Account

"However long the night, the dawn will break."—*African Proverb*

Have you ever been really tired, and then pushed yourself to go do something anyway? Perhaps it was dinner with a friend or attending a talk or lecture. Sometime during that event, the fatigue disappeared and was replaced by a second wind. That second wind is energy you produce. It isn't energy generated by food or sleep, but energy created chemically. Mihaly Csikszentmihalyi, author of the groundbreaking book Flow (1991), documented how fresh information—or a new interpretation—increases interest, drive, and energy. By changing our thinking, we can change our physical energy.

While believed to be true by many throughout the ages, the concept wasn't scientifically proven until recently. Originally, most scientists believed the relationship between the physical and emotional was a one-way street. The body influenced mood and thought, but thought and mood did not directly influence the body. Then, advanced brain-imaging techniques led to a startling discovery. The brain of a person *physically* doing something (i.e., playing basketball) looked almost identical to the person *thinking* about doing that activity. The same areas of the brain were stimulated. This explains why perception and outlook are a major factors in the energy equation. It isn't self-improvement mumbo jumbo, but an area where we truly can reclaim a lot of energy—once we learn how.

DISCOVERING EMOTIONAL ENERGY

To use emotional energy in your everyday life, you first need to discover what produces this energy *for you personally*. In your journal create a list of energy-producers, which you can populate as you discover them. Whenever you feel the need to rejuvenate emotional energy, look at your idea list. Here are a few that are on my list:

- Read positive feedback or notes I have received from readers
- Read a book that I find inspiring or motivational— something that really "speaks" to me
- Delve into a good literary novel
- Make sure I start my day off with positive emotional energy through my Good Morning routine
- Reading/writing poetry
- Devotional and prayer study
- Visual journaling and free-writing
- Digital collage and design
- Finding an hour to relax, give myself a facial without feeling rushed
- Anything creative—painting, scrapbooking, etc.
- Sitting outside on our porch
- Writing on my blog
- Throwing the Frisbee for the dog

Note: List activities you can do ALONE. People who rejuvenate our energy (and those that don't) are covered in the You've Gotta Have Friends Mini-Makeover.

On the next page of your journal make a list of items that drain emotional energy. Again, keep the focus on activities within your control. All stimuli influence our energy one way or the other. Watch for stimuli that negatively influence your energy level. Example: Watching a round of *Headline News* will catch you up on the day's headlines. But, does watching additional programming help or hinder? What about reading? Are your choices uplifting and inspiring more energy or are they energy sappers? What about music? Are you listening to uplifting songs or the latest forlorn love song?

TAKE A STEP FORWARD

For the next seven days, manage your emotional energy account. Whenever you do something that increases emotional energy record it in your journal. Each time you do something that drains your energy (you'll know these activities because you will literally feel your mood/emotions/energy taking a turn for the worse), record the activity. At the end of the seven-day period, "balance" the account. Did you spend more time on activities that increased or decreased your emotional energy? If you "overdraft" in this area, then you have uncovered one of the key drainers of energy — negative traps. Actively seek out time to make deposits into your emotional energy account through enjoyable activities.

Continue this practice until you are naturally more in balance. In the future if you feel the "weight of the world" on your shoulders or nagging gloom, revisit this Step.

TOOLS, RESOURCES, AND REFERENCES
  ☒ Reconcile your emotional energy account in your private online journal.

self and sanity step 4

Operation Handbag

"Taking joy in life is a woman's best cosmetic." —*Rosalind Russell*

Most women carry at least one bag, tote, briefcase, or purse. A well-packed handbag is more than an accessory; it is a command post that can help us stay organized, efficient, and sane. Giving your bag a functionality check and makeover can help you be well-prepared in any situation. With proper setup you can avoid uttering "I know it's in here somewhere..." while engaging in the eternal search for parking meter change, a pen, Advil, or lip balm.

For many years I carried the world's largest handbag. Weighing in at no less than twenty-five pounds, I believed I was prepared for every situation. Many shoulder aches later, I finally put together a system that allowed me to be prepared for any event while also maintaining a bag that would not require monthly chiropractic visits.

The "right" handbag is a must. I have two that I use regularly. One is a small purse, about seven by six inches with a long strap that can be securely slung over my head and under one arm. I use this bag when out with a small child, while traveling, and when running short errands so I can have both hands free.

My other bag is much larger, a cross between a hobo-style bag, tote, briefcase, and purse. It has short handles and a detachable strap. Most days this is the bag that accompanies me. I can fit my camera, a book, my CAN, my Catch-It envelope, entertainment for my daughter (hand-held game system, maze book), or even a toaster!

TOO MANY CLUB CARDS?
HERE ARE SOME SOLUTIONS:

At many stores you can give your phone number or membership number instead of showing your card. Type a list of store names along with your membership numbers, laminate and place in your wallet.

Use a hole-punch and punch a hole in the corner of each card. Place all the cards on a key ring, or make two key rings, one for frequently used cards and another for not-so-often used. Instead of adding this to your key chain, leave it in your purse. If you share these cards with a spouse or other adult, hang the ring where key chains are kept in the home. This ring system avoids having to weed through cards and disorganize a wallet each time a card is required. Cards are also easier to keep track of when they're all together.

The key to using multiple bags is to create an easy-transfer system. Think of your handbag as containing separate stations.

DOLLARS AND I.D.

The most common bag component is a wallet for securing money and identification. Take a peek in your wallet. Do you have anything besides money or identification inside? Many people find outdated receipts, twenty-two credit cards, a checkbook and register, expired membership cards, club cards for clubs we never visit, the family history in photos. Instead of managing these contents, many people buy a bigger wallet until the wallet is two or three inches thick, weighs five pounds, and cannot be closed!

To avoid overfilling your wallet, get the smallest functional wallet that you can find. Place only your identification, cash, and frequently used credit cards and club cards inside. If you have many other club cards, hole-punch the corners and put them on a key ring or keep them in a separate pouch. By keeping lesser-used cards separate you can quickly and easily condense into a smaller bag when needed. If you have very few cards or wallet items, consider looking for purses that have a zip pocket inside, and use this as the home for identification.

CHANGE YOUR WEIGHT

Coins carelessly strewn in a purse weigh it down quickly. Use a small zipper pouch to store coins so you can find them easily. Empty these coins into a jar at home regularly.

Secret Savings

For years I have used change as my "secret savings." Whenever I make a purchase, I pay with dollar bills and no coins. Even if the purchase is $10.02, I will give the cashier $11.00. I put my change into my bag and transfer it every other day into a large container at home. When the container is full, I take it to the bank and add it to my daughter's college savings. We are often amazed at how quickly this change adds up to hundreds of dollars!

COSMETICS

Have you ever emptied a purse and found several lipsticks at the bottom? Have you ever needed a specific cosmetic item and been unable to easily locate it in your purse? I solved this dilemma by keeping two or three small cosmetic bags with different looks (i.e., one for nighttime that's a bit more dramatic, one for day wear with warm colors, one for day wear with cool colors). In each small bag I have the following: mascara, pressed powder, eyeliner, lipliner, lipstick, eye shadow duo, blush, and undereye concealer. These bags are kept near my other cosmetics. When I get ready each morning, I grab the applicable bag and add it to my purse, then return it to my cosmetic area in the evening.

TO-DO STATIONS

If you are heading to a doctor's appointment or another location in which you will likely have some extra time, take your bigger bag and add something from your to-do pile. I keep an envelope in the kitchen near where I open my mail, and I put items I need to read or review inside. I often grab this when going to an appointment. I also keep blank note cards with a pen in a zipper-top plastic bag. When I go somewhere I can add this to my purse and catch up on writing notes and cards to friends.

OTHER ITEMS FOR YOUR HANDBAG:

- If you are a contact lens wearer, include a small bottle of solution, an extra pair of contact lenses, and an extra case (good to keep in a plastic bag in case of leakage)
- Sunglasses
- Hairbrush or comb
- One or two wet naps
- Your actual or a photocopy of your health insurance card and auto insurance card
- Emergency contact information (and who to notify in case of an accident); tuck this in your wallet or next to your ID.
- Small note pad
- If you take medications, a twenty-four-hour supply of your medicines in case you are unexpectedly stranded somewhere
- Pen
- Needle and thread (the small travel sewing kits you get at hotels work perfectly)
- Band-Aid or two
- Contact list of frequently called numbers (if you do not keep them in your cell phone)

Pack any of these items in small bags for your purse. The goal is to avoid loose items which make everything hard to find and hard to transfer. Instead, you'll have a combination of small bags that can be easily transferred from one carrier to another. You also won't have to spend an hour digging when the woman behind you in the "speedy-checkout" line is sighing condescendingly.

When choosing a station holder, opt for those with zippers to keep items in place. Be creative in the container hunt. I found many of my station holders within the home. Various cosmetic bags are a great place to check first!

TAKE A STEP FORWARD
Grab your handbag and dump out all the contents. Using the tips above, develop bags and small stations to store all of your items.

TOOLS, RESOURCES, AND REFERENCES
- ☑ Curious as to what lurks in my bags? View how I applied Operation Handbag to my life online.

self and sanity step 5

Girls' Night Out

"Each friend represents a world in us, a world possibly not born until they arrive, and it is only by this meeting that a new world is born." —*Anaïs Nin*

When I first created the Challenge, I spent a great deal of time examining those months in my life when I felt the most fulfilled. I looked for the common denominators among those periods. One thing I noticed was that during my most fulfilled times, I regularly had a "Girls' Night Out."

In my life, if I don't have a standing appointment, my best intentions to connect with others for enjoyment are often pushed aside by other demands. Intentions too often dissolve into "yesterdays." Over time, this lack of connection with other women can leave us feeling lonely or isolated. There is a unique dimension to female friendships that cannot be duplicated with relatives or men. Establishing a regular night (or afternoon) "out with the girls" guarantees a good laugh, adult conversation, and social time with a trusted circle.

When I lived in Portland, I was invited to join a "Bunco" group. Bunco is a very simple dice game anyone can learn in less than five minutes. The game requires little skill or focus, making it easy to *talk and share* while playing. In our group we had twenty women. The game is played by dividing into groups of four and then changing groups as the game progresses. This allowed everyone to visit throughout the night.

This is just one example. There are all sorts of groups to join or create—a book club, bowling league, craft club, walking group, to name a few. The process needn't be complicated; just find a group that appeals to you and dive in. If you cannot find a group, ask local schools, community centers, newspapers, or churches for ideas since these venues often announce group events. If you are struggling to find a group, you have likely identified a need within the community. Start a group of your own. Other women are likely looking for a group too! Consider starting a small group using the *Change Your Life Challenge* program.

TAKE A STEP FORWARD

Aim to have at least two nights per month (weekly if possible) in which time is spent visiting with a group of women. Women can learn a lot from one another, share in unique ways, and support one another. Within the next twenty-four hours, schedule a Girls' Night Out. If you cannot find or decide on a group within that time, just arrange a get together at a local café with several women friends. Then work to solidify your Girls' Night Out plans in the next two weeks.

TOOLS, RESOURCES, AND REFERENCES
⊠ Join me for a "Girls' Night Out Online." Hosted monthly in our online chat room, these "Girls' Nights" cover a variety of topics, guest speakers, game tournaments, and end with a bit of pampering (like a recipe for a homemade spa treatment.)
☑ Twice a year I host a free "Girls' Night Out Online." Sign up to receive a reminder at the website.

mini-makeover

Money Matters

"The only reason a great many American families don't own an elephant is that they have never been offered an elephant for a dollar down and easy weekly payments." —*Mad Magazine*

Almost unanimously, women rate finances as a top stressor. When finances are tight, attitude and outlook are affected. But no matter where you are financially, there are steps that can put you on the road to financial freedom. This Mini-Makeover will help you change your thinking about money, manage day-to-day spending, and overcome impulse spending once and for all.

Step 1: Determining Your Value Number

Step 2: Why We Buy: Silly Ways We Lose Money and How to Stop

Step 3: Create a Spending Diary

Step 4: Managing Day-to-Day Spending

Step 5: The Impulse Spending Solution

Supply List:
- Stapler or Scotch tape
- 6 – 9 x 12 paper envelopes
- 10 standard white #10 envelopes (or other small envelopes on hand)

money matters step 1

Discovering Your Value Number

"It's good to have money and the things that money can buy, but it's good, too, to check up once in a while and make sure you haven't lost the things that money can't buy." —*George Horace Lorimer*

For many, the following simple exercise can be as effective as budgeting. Think of money in terms of life's energy. This idea of taking your income, subtracting the cost of working, and dividing that number by the hours you work in a year is a concept developed by Vicki Robin, best-selling author of Your Money or Your Life. If you are married you would use your combined family income. If you do not work outside of the home, use the hours you work inside the home and your combined family income.

Here is an example of how this works. Julie makes $26,000 a year gross. After taxes and her IRA she has $18,000 left. Day care totals $7,280.00 annually. She commutes fifteen miles to work each way. At the government rate of .315 cents a mile, that's $2340.00 annually. Julie eats lunch out about twice a week and her average meals costs $7.00; to that we add two sodas and a coffee. These food expenses total $1170.00 for the year. Between dry cleaning, clothes, and pantyhose she spends an additional $960 each year. (Remember, we're just analyzing the cost of working).

Subtract these amounts from Julie's net income and she is left with $6250.00 per year. Divide that by the 2000 hours she works and she is netting $3.12 per hour. Knowing this number is the best way to spend less without budgeting. Here's how:

According to Robin, you need to ask yourself, "Is this item worth this much of my life energy?" The next time you are looking at a $30.00 shirt, ask yourself, "Is this shirt worth ten hours (or six hours, or 14 hours) of my time?" If it is, buy it; if it isn't, don't. Ask yourself this of everything you purchase.

Let's look at another example, in which one parent works outside the home and the other works within the home caring for two young children.

- Father's outside work hours: sixty hours
- Commuting time: six hours
- Mother's work-at-home hours: fifty-five hours
- Commuting time — three hours (running kids, errands)
- Father's income: $65,000 after taxes
- Father's work expenses total: $6,000 (dry cleaning, mileage, work clothes, meals)
- After-expense income: $59,000
- Total hours worked between both spouses: 115 (or 5980 per year)
- Average hourly income $9.86 for combined or $4.93 for each work hour by mother or father

How many hours of life energy are you willing to lose?

TAKE A STEP FORWARD

Today, figure out your own "value number." Begin by taking your annual gross income and then subtract the following (if you share financials with another person, use your combined income):

Gross Income   _____

Net Income after Taxes   _____

All work associated expenses   _____

**(Include mileage, dry cleaning,
    food, coffees, etc.)**   _____

After-expense income _____

Number of hours worked per year _____

Divide the number of worked hours into the after-expense income, this equals

Value Number _____

Begin asking: "Is this item worth this much of my life energy?" when making a purchase. File a copy of this worksheet behind the Money Matters tab in the Headquarters.

money matters step 2

WHY WE BUY
Silly Ways We Lose Money
and How to Stop

"There was a time when a fool and his money were soon parted, but now it happens to everybody."—*Adlai E. Stevenson*

The campaigns of advertisers and marketers aim to stir one or more of the following beliefs:
- The item or service will create more time
- The item or service will help to save or create more money
- The item or service will enhance or create happiness
- The item or service will create or enhance beauty/physical appearance
- The item or service will decrease stress, worry, anxiety, or other undesirable feelings and emotions

One or more of these five core needs is on almost everyone's need list.

It is a cycle. A consumer is exposed to an ad, whether it is on television, in a magazine, over the radio, on a billboard, or in the mail. The ad that is read, seen, or heard has been written by a highly-paid individual well-versed at identifying universal driving factors.

Perhaps there is evidence of this in your own home. Look for items that you have purchased but that have gone unused or rarely used. For each item ask: "What benefit did I believe I would receive?" Did the purchase create that benefit: more time, money, beauty, happiness, or less stress?

SILLY WAYS WE LOSE MONEY AND HOW TO STOP

Pay special attention to what type of items you purchase the most. This observation will help determine your highest susceptibility for impulse purchasing while also revealing an area of your life that needs a thorough real-life solution. Spend some time journaling about possible ways you could create less stress, more time, more beauty (or whatever category your items fall into) without buying anything. We have the personal ability to create much of what we need without any purchased items. The quick-fix lure can be tempting, but in the long run it doesn't challenge us to uncover what we truly need and/or how we can contribute to that need internally.

IF ONE IS GOOD, TWO MUST BE BETTER

I do a lot of expo shows around the country. An expo show is basically a gathering of vendors that are selling their products. I am usually there to do a speaking engagement or to sign books. One of the most common marketing tactics I see at these expos is the "two-item upsell."

I first noticed this at a cooking expo. Almost every woman that passed my booth was carrying two large mops. For every ninety-nine women that had two mops, there was one woman that had a single mop. My curiosity peaking, I finally asked a woman what the mops were about.

Basically, after watching a fairly impressive demo, people could purchase a mop for $20 and get a second mop for only $5 more. This is a common marketing tactic. One can quickly do the math in your head—one mop for $20 or two mops for only $12.50 each. Clearly the better "deal" is two mops at $12.50. But do all of these women truly need two mops? Perhaps those with large homes or multiple stories could benefit from two—but I can't believe that every woman fell into that category. Plus, each mop came with its own lifetime guarantee!

Our minds can justify this type of purchase in other ways: "This is so cool, now I'll have a spare." "What if I love this product and want to get another one and can't find it?" "I'll give the second mop to _____." The goal of marketing and advertising is to get us to think in that way.

TWO FOR $10

This one is often seen at supermarkets. Two items are on sale for a low price, or four items are on sale for a low price with your Club Card. Once, I found a cereal I wanted to try listed at four boxes for $8.00—almost 50 percent savings! The problem was I didn't know if I liked the cereal. If I didn't like it, this would result in a pretty big loss. Here's the trick: I went up to customer service and asked if I still received the savings with a one-box purchase and the answer was yes. I have asked this question many times when seeing these special deals and almost always you can buy one at the same price as the bulk special. Most of the software running supermarket sales is configured that way.

DISORGANIZATION

How many times have you bought something you already owned because you could not find the item when needed? Common examples are tweezers, clippers, scissors, and sunglasses; add your own to the list.

I resolved to stop this loss pattern after my last trip to Disney World. The parks sell those bottles that mist water with an electric fan, which can be a life-saver in the heat. The only drawback is that they cost $17.00. However, they quickly turn a child who is grumbling about the weather into a happy child. I have made six trips to Disney. Each time I have forgotten the bottle we purchased on a previous trip. I have spent over $100 on these fan/water bottles, which is kind of silly seeing that we live in Wisconsin and would not have any use for them outside of Florida.

The list goes on. While I am not a fanny-pack person, I do wear one at Disney to keep everything dry and organized, and to avoid carrying a camera bag or purse. Since wearing fanny-packs is otherwise foreign to me, for each of the six trips I have bought a $25 fanny pack in the parks. (I always get the one that says GRUMPY).

To solve this, I now have a designated "Disney travel bag" stored with my other luggage. Whenever we return from Disney World I place the water bottle, fanny pack, and any Disney-necessities inside so as not to forget them on the next trip!

THE VALUE-PACKED DEAL

Have you ever flipped through a magazine and had an annoying ad card fall out? Then you glance at the card and realize that you just spent three dollars for a magazine that could have been delivered to your home each month for only $10 annually. The card might also feature a bonus tote bag, pamphlet, or other add-on making it a "smart choice" to subscribe—after all you could save 90 percent!

Years ago, my house was overflowing from the magazines I ordered off of these cards (that must be why they put so many of them in the magazines). Interestingly, I realized that after a couple of issues the magazines often became clutter, stacked in various places with the hopes I'll find time to read them. The piles got bigger and bigger, but my time to page through them did not grow in proportion. In the end, this financial "savings" causes day-to-day paper-management stress.

Note: Take a look at the subscriptions you receive now. Do you read the magazines or do you stack them unread like I do? If you only read one or two issues a year, it is better to avoid the clutter and buy them at the newsstand. Plus, many magazines now offer all or some content online.

BUY NOW PAY LATER, A.K.A. TAKE HOME NOW, HAVE A HEADACHE LATER

Furniture and computer stores are famous for their sales that let you buy now and don't pay for X years. Even though we may not have the money to pay cash now, we somehow are comfortable enough to assume we will have it later. I don't know about you, but nine times out of ten I have not had the money magically appear later. And when the money isn't there, the interest charges begin, often making the item cost two to three times its original list price.

Let's say I purchased a $5,000 bedroom set on a pay-later plan, and the interest rate was 14 percent (which isn't bad in today's interest-laden traps). If I made the minimum payments, assuming they are around 1.5 percent of the outstanding balance, it would take sixty-one years to pay off the bedroom set and cost close to $16,000 in interest.

Taking a moment to do the "worst-case-scenario" math is a very good exercise before purchasing on these plans. Compare your findings to your Value Number. How many hours of life energy would the item really cost? After doing this exercise, I found saving up and paying cash much more appealing and rewarding.

PLEASE, MOM! PARENTING GUILT

When we don't have as much quality time as we would like with our children, we can easily be susceptible to buying "bonus gifts" or "treats." Setting limits and rules on child-spending helps teach children boundaries and the value of money—and avoids the "gimme gimme" cycle.

PERCEIVED VALUE

Another marketing ploy is perceived value and convenience. The goal of this type of ad is to make you think that by having a specific item within arm's reach you will be able to save money. Some good examples of this are: espresso machines, home-gym systems, ab-rollers, bread machines, pasta makers, etc.

Some people will actually use these purchases regularly and for those people the savings will be dramatic. Yet, most of the population will purchase these items because of a perceived value and benefit and not use them.

I know of several people (myself included) who have spent hundreds on an espresso machine. The logic was that a barista coffee can cost $3 to $5. If you have one a day, that is $100 per month. In three months you pay for the machine and save money thereafter, right? Well, unless you're like me. I discovered that not being the person to make the coffee was a large portion of what I enjoyed.

While technically the espresso machine would have saved money, it did not offer the experience I enjoyed and I rarely used it.

It's likewise with gym equipment: many people need the routine of going to a gym and the support system provided there, and are less likely to use purchased equipment at home.

Before purchasing a perceived-value item, make sure it is something you will use.

TAKE A STEP FORWARD

Think through the questions below thoroughly. Write down the questions and your answers on some blank paper and add them to the spending journal we will create in the next step.

- Identify the areas where you are most susceptible to marketing and advertising. What are some other ways you could improve in these areas—without purchasing anything?
- Can you think of any times where you have succumbed to "If one is good, two must be better?"
- Think about what items you have repurchased due to disorganization. Make a common and easily accessible "housing area" for these items.
- How often do you buy the displayed sale number—i.e., two for $10 or four for $20 versus buying what you actually need? Do you ever lose money this way? Which products make sense to purchase this way? Which products don't? While you may be able to get four rolls of aluminum foil for 50 percent savings—how long will it take to use them? Does purchasing like this leave you short on cash? If we have a cash surplus, these stock up opportunities often make sense, but if we are living paycheck to paycheck, we should purchase for the next ninety days maximum.
- What magazines do you actually read each month? Write those below. When magazine renewal notices come your way, avoid renewing those not on this list.

- Have you purchased items based on perceived-value without considering the routine and experience involved? List any below and what you discovered.
- Does parenting guilt play a role in your impulse purchases? What effective ways can you brainstorm to set limits on spending with children? Remember, consistency is key when working with kids.
- When have you bought something now to pay later? Write down an example or two and calculate the "true cost" and "life energy hours" you ended up using.

money matters step 3

Create a Spending Station

"Failing to plan is planning to fail."—Alan Lakein

A Spending Station is a control center for managing finances efficiently. The Station created in this Mini-Makeover has three categories, each with its own envelope: bills, wants, and actual spending. In this Step we set up the Spending Station and cover the Wants envelope.. The next Step will guide you through how to use the Spending Station to effectively manage day-to-day finances.

Gather the six 9 x 12 envelopes and set them up as follows:

- **Wants:** Create one envelope by stapling or taping the Wants Ledger to the envelope.
- **Bills:** This envelope will take the place of the bills envelope in Step 15. Make a photocopy of the Bill Ledger or print from the website. List all of your recurring bills on the ledger. Include the date due but not the month. For example, instead of listing March 1 as the due date for a mortgage, write "the 1st." Make several photocopies of this worksheet and keep the original as a "Master." Tuck it behind the Money Matters tab in your Headquarters. Staple three photocopies to three separate envelopes. Write the current month at the top of one envelope, and label the other two envelopes with the two upcoming months.
- **Actual Spending:** Create two envelopes by stapling or taping the Spending Ledger to the envelopes. Date one

Wants List

Item (include description, item #, SKU)	Date Seen	Purchased after 30 days?	Amount Spent (if purchased)	Amount Saved (if not purchased))
		Y N		
		Y N		
		Y N		
		Y N		
		Y N		
		Y N		
		Y N		
		Y N		
		Y N		
		Y N		
		Y N		
		Y N		
		Y N		
		Y N		
		Y N		
		Y N		
		Y N		
		Y N		
		Total		

Bills Ledger _____

Due Date	Amount	Company Name	Date Paid	Check Number	Confirmation Number

Spending Ledger _____

Date	Amount	Company Name	Want or Need?	Source and Confirmation Number	Balance

envelope with the current month, and the other with the upcoming month.

- **Important:** Do not glue the ledger worksheets to the envelopes.

No Assembly Required

Visit our online store at www.brooknoelstudio.com for ready-made color envelopes

Add these envelopes to the other action envelopes created in Step 15: Nightly Reflection.

THE WANT ENVELOPE, A.K.A. YOUR PERSONAL LAY-AWAY PLAN

Putting a stop on impulse buying is one of the quickest ways to regain control of your finances. Spending an extra $10 or $20 when you go to a Costco, Wal-Mart or the grocery store adds up to thousands over time. The goal of this section is not a deprivation plan, but to encourage careful consideration of purchases. Consider it your personal no-money-down lay-away system.

Whenever you find a nonessential item that you want, add it to the Want Ledger. (If you aren't at home, write it in your CAN and transfer during your Nightly Reflection.) Include the item or SKU number if you can. If it is from a catalog or an online store, print a page of the item detail and tuck it in the envelope. (If you decide to purchase the item, this information will allow you to do so quickly.) Make sure to also record the date you discovered the item on the Want Ledger.

The Want List has a mandatory "Thirty-Day Hold." After thirty days from the recorded date, if you still want to purchase the item and have the funds to do so—go for it. I think you will be amazed at how many items don't seem so desirable (some even seem silly) after a thirty-day cool off period. Use the far two columns to mark whether you end up purchasing the item or not. When you have filled an entire "Want" page, total how much money you saved by not purchasing items after a thirty-day period. The results will likely encourage you to use this incubation as a lifetime practice in making smart buying decisions.

Note: There will be occasional out-of-the-ordinary situations requiring a purchase within thirty days—a needed gift or an unexpected event for which you need something specific to attend. These are "needs," not "wants," and should be recorded in the Actual Spending envelope covered in the next Step. Keep exceptions to this Thirty-Day Hold rule to a minimum or put a "max limit" on how much you can spend.

TAKE A STEP FORWARD

Set up your Spending Station by creating the wants, bills, and actual-spending envelopes. Gather any current wants and add to the wants envelope following the instructions in this Step. Create a master ledger for bills and make several photocopies to create actual-spending envelopes.

TOOLS, RESOURCES, AND REFERENCES
    ☑ Additional copies of all the worksheets in this section can be printed from the website; ready-made envelopes are also available.

money matters step 4

Managing Day-to-Day Spending

"Too many people spend money they haven't earned, to buy things they don't want, to impress people they don't like." —*Will Rogers*

With the Wants category set up, adding the actual spending and bills categories creates a "financial hub" for your life. When all three of these sections are in place, tracking bills, wants, needs, and spending can be centralized into one manageable system.

BILLS ENVELOPE

When processing your Catch-It Collectors, continue the practice learned in Step 15. For any bills, record the due date and the bill information if it is not already on your master list. Throw away any extra flyers, offers, or paper accompanying the bill. Place the bill and the return envelope in one of the financial envelopes depending on *the date it is due.*

ACTUAL-SPENDING ENVELOPE

The actual-spending envelope is an all-in-one finance register and file system. Each month this envelope collects all the details and records of need-based, want-based, and actual (or unexpected) spending. Unlike a check register which only records transactions for a checking account, the actual spending envelopes records all purchases—credit cards, cash, and checking. The payment method column on the worksheet is for indicating the money source, such as debit card, personal checking, American Express, or cash.

MAINTAINING YOUR RECORDS

Whenever you empty the Catch-It Collectors (Make Time Matter Step 4) place receipts in the actual spending envelope and record them on the ledger. Add bills to the Bills envelope.

Once each week sit down with your Spending Station envelopes and make sure all activity has been recorded by using the following checklist:

1. Check your Catch-All Notebook for any items that need to be written down on the Want list. Review any entries on this list that are thirty days old to decide whether you will purchase them or not and note your choice on the worksheet.
2. Check the need-based overview for any upcoming bills. Find the bills in the Needs envelope. Write any checks or make payments and record them on the actual-spending ledger. Place the portion you retain of the bill (if any) in the actual-spending envelope for reference.
3. Make sure all receipts are recorded on the actual-spending worksheet. If you find many of the receipts are unexpected expenses, begin starring unexpected expenses to see how they add up each month. Set a limit for these unexpected expenses. If you continually exceed the limit, you would benefit from a detailed budget plan.

At the end of each month:

1. Total up your Want ledger. Notice how much you saved. If there are any items you would like to purchase, do so if the month wait is up. Remove any items you no longer want and cross them off the Want ledger so the envelope is current for the new month. Whenever you complete a want ledger, remove it from the envelope and attach a new one. File the

existing want ledger behind the Money Matters tab in your Headquarters.

2. Remove the actual-spending ledger from the envelope and place it behind the Money Matters tab in your CYLC Headquarters. Label the envelope with the month and year in larger lettering. File the actual spending envelope in a cabinet or box. If you need to locate a receipt for any reason, the actual-spending ledger in the Headquarters will provide a quick reference for which envelope to look in.

3. All paid bills should have been recorded in your actual-spending envelope. Any unpaid bills should be transferred to the next month's bill envelope.

I store my warranties and instruction manuals in the actual-spending envelope for the month the purchase was made. The actual-spending ledger in my Headquarters makes it easy to find what I need when I need it.

TAKE A STEP FORWARD
Begin using the full Spending Station to actively manage your finances.

TOOLS, RESOURCES, AND REFERENCES

☒ Download the member e-book *A Checklist for Financial Freedom: Ideas for Everyday Savings* for more ideas to manage your money wisely.

☑ Need to create a full budget? Visit the website to learn about my *Busy Woman's Budgeting Toolkit,* which comes with a workbook, budget book, and computer software for budgeting.

money matters step 5

The Impulse-Spending Solution

"The quickest way to double your money is to fold it over and put it back in your pocket." — *Will Rogers*

I once had twelve credit cards with balances that would make most people's head spin (and they did make my and my husband's spin). In addition to the credit cards, we had two revolving lines of credit. No longer—now I have a debit card and an American Express card for traveling, which is paid in full every thirty days. I reject all credit offers and do not buy anything I cannot pay for at the time of purchase.

While this change of habits was difficult and I often longed for a fallback or a card with no interest for X days, it has greatly reduced my stress and our stress as a couple when it comes to finances. (Getting here was a long haul…tens of thousands upon thousands upon thousands of debt to pay off first.) This change of habits also allowed us to quit buying into commercialism, stress, and living beyond our means.

When we first transitioned from credit to cash, we used an envelope system. I made a list of budget categories we paid in person, for example groceries, car fuel and maintenance, dry cleaning, and entertainment. We decided how much money we would allot to each category. I totaled these amounts and then withdrew that amount of cash from the bank. I separated the cash into #10 envelopes by category. Throughout the week we would take money from the specific envelope to cover our expenses. Receipts were returned to the envelopes, or if we didn't have a receipt we made a note about how much we spent and where. If the envelope was empty by midweek we did not take out more cash. Instead, we either waited for the following week or reduced spending in another category to cover the shortage. Any money left over at week's end was "fun money."

TAKE A STEP FORWARD

If impulse-purchasing or overspending is causing financial stress, create your own envelope system using the envelopes from this Mini-Makeover supply list. Maintain the system for a minimum of four weeks to begin seeing results.

mini-makeover

Family Matters

"A hundred years from now it will not matter what my bank account was, the sort of house I lived in, or the kind of car I drove...but the world may be different because I was important in the life of a child."—*Anonymous*

In today's hectic world, managing day-to-day family matters can seem more difficult than putting a man on Mars. This Mini-Makeover shares strategies for handling common errands, using chore and reward systems with kids (or for you!), and keeping a well-bonded family unit.

Step 1: Operating the Errand Express

Step 2: Do unto Others...

Step 3: Host a Happy Half Hour

Step 4: Who is that Person across the Table?

Step 5: Chore and Reward Systems that Work

family matters step 1

Operating the Errand Express

"If you chase two rabbits, both will escape."—*Proverb*

How many times have you arrived home only to realize something you intended to pick up or do was forgotten during the day? With packed schedules and filled minds, multitasking throughout the day is difficult at best.

Operating the Errand Express can eliminate spinning your wheels, wasted time, endless family requests for "one little favor," in addition to saving money, reducing stress, and allowing the focus needed to get the job done versus always feeling like something has been forgotten.

Think of the Errand Express as a special service company you own and operate. The only caveat is, the cost to run the Errand Express is high, so it cannot operate twenty-four hours a day, seven days a week, or on demand. The Errand Express only operates on a limited half- or full-day schedule.

Begin by writing down the errands you do currently and how often these errands are done. Use this list to estimate how much time to schedule for the Errand Express. Depending on how many errands you have, choose a full or half day and block off the hours you will use for running errands. Depending on the hours you are available, you may want or need to split errand time into two time blocks, for example split a half day between two hours on Monday and three hours on Saturday. Consider traffic, family schedules, and store crowdedness when setting your schedule.

Errand Tracking

Errand	MON	TUE	WED	THU	FRI	SAT	SUN	NUM OF WEEKS PER MONTH

Instructions:
Group errands on separate worksheets depending on frequency, i.e. weekly, monthly. Use the far right column to note how often each errand is done, i.e. 1 week each month, every week.

Double check your list to make sure it includes all of your errands. The goal is to consolidate all errands into Errand Express time and not to veer from the schedule unless it is an emergency; for example, prescriptions to be filled for a sick child.

SORTING ERRANDS

Sort your errand list into logical groups. Group errands by how frequently they are done; for example: weekly or monthly. Make a separate checklist for weekly and monthly errands, writing the errands to be done in a logical sequence based on location (this will help avoid driving in circles). If errands are split between family members, make a separate checklist for each family member. Match the grouped errands to your calendar to determine the best time to operate the Errand Express. You will likely have a weekly route, monthly route, and other routes requiring different stops. Keep these master lists behind the Routines tab in your Headquarters.

GET THE FAMILY ON BOARD

Take a blank piece of paper (or use the worksheet in the Companion Workbook) and write the scheduled day and time at the top; for example, Monday, 12:00 p.m. to 5:00 p.m. Write the "stop" (grocery store, dry cleaner, discount store, gas station, hardware store, pharmacy, post office) and then leave a space for family members to write in requests. Make sure to add an "other" stop for any miscellaneous errands. Secure this schedule to the front of the refrigerator.

EXPLAIN THE SYSTEM

Give family members a week or two of notice about the new Errand Express service. Explain all requests need to be written down on the provided sheet to help you accomplish them efficiently. Make it clear items not on the list will not be done until the following week—at least not by you—unless, of course, it's an emergency.

Encourage people to write down any food or household items they use the last of (or notice getting low) on the errand sheet (this is why it is kept on the refrigerator).

DESIGNATE A PICK-UP LOCATION

Some errands will require drop-off services; for example, dry cleaning or mailing a package. Choose a spot for family members to place items the night before or day of the Errand Express. I have a large plastic tub in the laundry room for bulky items and dry cleaning, and then an envelope for any paper items. Let family members know the pick-up location and explain that all items must be present for the errand to be done. Writing an errand on the list is not enough if there are items you will need to complete the errand. When you drop-off anything, make a note in the Active Task List in your CAN to add pick-up (if needed) to a future Errand Express schedule.

HOW THIS HELPS

Time: Due to lack of planning, many people run the same errand, or pass the same location dozens of times each week resulting in lost money (gas) and time. Even if it is "just a ten-minute trip" here and there, it adds up to days over the course of a year.

Money: The more times we enter any retail building, the more times we are likely to buy something. If we have another person with us, the likelihood doubles.

Focus: Instead of sidetracking your day, errands can be done effectively with focus.

Quality time: Instead of spending hours going in circles for multiple family members, we can spend more quality time with family.

WHAT IF?

I have had a few women tell me the Errand Express would not work for their family. I always ask if they have tried the Step and they always reply, "No." Often, these women express feelings of guilt and assume they would be inconveniencing a husband or children by reducing errand availability time. After referring them back to the Give Up the Cape Step, I ask: "If I knew someone who would like to help you for several hours each week with anything you need as long as you write down what it is you need, and she would do this for you pleasantly and at no cost, how would you respond?" The answers range from leaping for joy to a capital-YES. "But isn't that an inconvenience?" They quickly draw the parallel between the Errand Express and the question I asked. I encourage them to share the idea with the family before saying it won't work. Many women are very glad they did.

TAKE A STEP FORWARD

Create your errand list and divide it into groups and set the date for the grand opening of the Errand Express.. Then follow the instructions to post and share with family members. On errand day, take the list with you. You may wish to keep completed lists for reference or to revise the master errand lists placed behind the Routines Tab earlier in this Step.

family matters step 2

Do unto Others...

"Your children will see what you're all about by what you live rather than what you say." —*Wayne Dyer*

Relationships are vital to our emotional well-being. The examples we set in our homes and our lives send a strong message to others, especially our children. What messages do your interactions send to your children? Are you positive, encouraging, and supporting in good times and bad? Are you quick-tempered or demanding? If you are married or in a relationship, is your relationship a good model for future relationships your child might have? Think of (or write down) three answers for each of the following questions in your journal

- The way I treat my children teaches...
- The way I handle difficult situations teaches...
- The way my partner and I handle problems together teaches...
- My schedules and priorities teach...
- The way (and frequency) I express love and affection teaches...
- The way I treat myself teaches...
- The way I treat and interact with my friends teaches...

While meeting the demands of day-to-day life, many people find the "little things" slip away. I recently read an essay about an elderly man reflecting on his life. If he could do it all over again, he wrote, he would focus more on the little things and less on the big things. In his old age, he realized the "big things" were comprised of all the "little things" he was too busy to be attentive to.

Below are some "little things" that mean a lot. Read them through, paying special attention for those that resonate most with you.

SHOW AFFECTION

Affection, touch, and words of support have proven to be of significant importance to both our physical and emotional well-being. Use nonverbal communication and touch to express appreciation, love, and warmth.

RESOLVE DISAGREEMENTS

When conflicts arise, allow enough time for participants to calm down, but do not leave it unresolved. As soon as everyone is composed, work it through to a fair resolution. Walking away or burying a conflict "under the rug" teaches children to hide, fear, or avoid conflict versus resolving it in a healthy way.

WRITE A NOTE

Write a thank you or appreciation note to your family. Tuck it in a child's backpack or lunch bag or in your spouse's coat pocket or brief case.

STOP

Give a person your undivided attention. Do not ask him to wait five minutes, do not listen while also reading or looking at a computer screen. (See Part Two, Step 8: The Five-Minute Relationship Miracle.)

SAY "YES" INSTEAD OF "NO"

As parents, we often get so used to saying "no" to protect young children or maintain limits that we begin saying it out of habit. Say "yes" at least once each day to something fun with your child. Make a snow angel. Take time to color. Do your best impersonation of an ape. Have fun.

REMAIN THE ADULT

Our children are specifically programmed with the ability to push our buttons within a millisecond. As children grow into adolescents and teens, this ability improves. Do not be surprised if a child provokes you. Instead, surprise your child by not taking the bait. Count to ten (or ten million). Doing so diffuses the situation and discourages further button-pushing.

SMILE

A famous quote reads, "The shortest distance between two people is a smile." Smiles and laughter create bonds, dissolve walls, and encourage communication. Trust me, there will be time to worry, be anxious, upset, or feel stress later; take a break from it at home.

ADMIT WHEN YOU ARE WRONG

When you are wrong or make a mistake, admit it. Avoid confrontational words like always, never, if you had, but, you should. Not only is it okay to be wrong, it is admirable when you can promptly admit it and apologize.

FOLLOW THROUGH

When you commit to a family member, follow through. Be on time. Finish projects you take on. Call if running behind. Doing so shows caring and respect.

TAKE A STEP FORWARD

Write down the "little things" that resonate with you on index cards to add to your Personal Power Deck. Choose one to keep in your CAN this week and work with daily.

TOOLS, RESOURCES, AND REFERENCES

☒ For more tips on handling day-to-day tasks, listen to or download my online audio, "Solutions for Hectic Households."

family matters step 3

Host a Happy Half Hour

"Life is what we make it. Always has been, always will be."—*Grandma Moses*

Adults have long reaped the gratification that "Happy Hour" can bring. Happy hour is that great time of day signifying work is done and we can relax, sit back, and enjoy focused time with friends.

Today, parents spend an average of seventeen minutes of quality time with children. Partners spend even less quality time together. Fifty years ago, families would sit down at least twice per day together over meals. Many families have lost the "anchors" connecting them to one another. Many of the challenges families face are compounded by a lack of unity within the home. Unity requires us to spend time with, enjoy, and support one another.

Once everyone is home (or if that is impossible due to shift work, when the majority of people are home) set out simple appetizers and beverages. Chips, peanuts, popcorn, fruit slices, grapes—any simple finger food will do. Sit back, relax, and enjoy one another. Ask and listen about each other's day. Learn something new about one another. Pick a random question and take turns answering it, for example, "If you could go anywhere on vacation for one week where would you go?"

If you do not have children, spend this time with your partner. If you do not have a partner, invite someone over to connect with, meet someone on a regular basis for enriched quality social time, or join us in the Action Jam Room online.

TAKE A STEP FORWARD

Tonight, surprise your family with a "happy half hour." Keep conversation light, upbeat, and encouraging.

family matters step 4

Who Is That Person across the Table?

"I used to think that being nice to people and feeling nice was loving people. Now I know it isn't. Love is the most immense unselfishness and it is so big I've never touched it."—Florence Allshom

A recent article in a popular woman's magazine compared the life of a married woman with children to the life of a single woman without kids. In the article the married woman said something to the effect that once you have children there is little time for your spouse. You just hope that when the kids are grown and gone, you married someone you will still want to spend time with.

At the time, the statement resonated deeply with me. My marriage had lost its spark and I could feel us drifting further and further apart. I had been sitting at the table, watching my husband as he ate, wondering: *who is that person?* With the demands of work, children, and life in general, the familiarity we shared had been replaced by distance. Our lives were changing and evolving rapidly, yet we had not kept each other informed on many of the changes we felt individually. We took for granted that we knew each other, and had not invested the time required to stay close.

I shared my feelings with my husband and learned he also shared my concerns but had been unsure how to reach out. Later as we talked, we learned we had both felt this way for months, yet ironically neither of us had the time or energy to bring it up, which only compounded the distance. We made the decision to actively reconnect. Here are some ideas that worked for us and may work for you.

TAKE WORK HOME

Both my husband and I had heard the rule of leaving work at the door and not taking it home. With many parents often working forty-hour weeks, sixty-hour weeks, or longer, work accounts for half of our waking hours. By not sharing this time, we cut out a huge piece of our experience. Your partner should know what is going on at work, who you like, the funny story. Help your partner understand the joys and frustrations that influence you daily.

MAKE A DATE

Regardless of what planets you need to move or miracles you must perform, go on a date at least every other week. It does not matter if you go out for breakfast, lunch, dinner, or a walk—just make sure that every other week you *connect* without children.

EXPRESS YOUR NEEDS

Teamwork is the glue of a successful marriage. When we can anticipate our partner's needs and offer our help, we make the days easier. Let your partner know how he can help you and find out how you can help him. Never assume that "he should just know." Express your needs clearly. Likewise, do not assume you understand his needs—ask. Nagging and disappointment can be drastically reduced by actively expressing ourselves versus being passive and expecting our partner to be psychic.

CREATE GOALS TOGETHER

Share your dreams and ambitions. Create common goals that you can work toward together. Goals create focus, communication, and shared vision. Set goals as a couple and as a family.

TAKE A STROLL DOWN MEMORY LANE

While living in the present and working toward the future, remember to relish the past. Page through an old photo album or recall favorite memories, journeys, and stories from the past.

HOLD HANDS

Affection, touch, and words of support have proven to be of significant importance to both our physical and emotional well-being. Hold hands, show affection. Choose to fill silence with words of support.

DWELL ON THE POSITIVE

Instead of focusing on the qualities your partner does not have or what he does not do, focus on the positive. Recall the qualities that drew you to him in the first place. Focus on the positive to perpetuate growth and appreciation.

THANK YOUR PARTNER REGULARLY

Many experts agree that marriages naturally fade a bit after several years. I believe much of this comes from a couple's choice (whether intentional or not) to stop doing the "little things" that were done in the early years of the relationship. Many spouses feel taken for granted by their partner. Saying "thank you" and expressing appreciation through a kind gesture, card, or email goes a long way. Reinstitute the extra level of caring found in a relationship's early years.

MAKE DAILY TIME TO CONNECT

Even if it is just five minutes while brushing your teeth, find a daily time to touch base, compare notes, and share ideas. The length of time is not important, but having a daily connection is vital to a healthy relationship. Much can happen in a single day. When we skip one day we are also likely to skip another, then another, until we find ourselves feeling isolated from our partner.

TAKE A STEP FORWARD

Stop for a moment and put down this book. Call and find a sitter or relative to watch your children and make a date with your partner. Write it down on the calendar and plan a fun time together. Try to do this every two weeks and take turns planning the date.

If you are not currently in a relationship: Don't think you are off the hook for today's assignment. You need to make sure that you are spending quality time with other people as well; take today to book a "date" with a friend.

family matters step 5

Chore and Reward
Systems That Work

"Man is always more than he can know of himself; consequently, his accomplishments, time and again, will come as a surprise to him."—*Golo Mann*

The family is a team and each family member a player. While children might feel parents are on an opposite team when requesting kids do chores or go to bed, children need to know that all family members wear the same jersey. It is a parent's responsibility to become an effective coach of the family team. Set boundaries, expectations, rules, and share responsibilities. When bumps come, don't give up. The key to effective coaching is clarity and consistency.

Chore and reward systems can be an incredibly effective family tool and beneficial to children. A good system inspires children while also teaching responsibility and discipline. I have never given my daughter an allowance, nor has she asked for one. We are both pleased with the chore and reward system and the teamwork it creates.

THE BASICS

A chore and reward system is a visual tool that lets children perform household tasks in order to earn something they would really like. Make a list of what you need help with. What would you like to delegate around the house? Cleaning up after dinner? Does laundry or dusting make you cringe? What about taking out garbage or mowing the lawn? Write down any age-appropriate responsibilities you would like to hand over to someone else.

ASK YOUR CHILD TO THINK OF AN ITEM HE OR SHE WOULD REALLY, REALLY LIKE

Find a picture of this item and place it on a piece of paper. Using your list of tasks create a "road" of squares leading to the item. Write one task within each square. Whenever a task is completed have the child date and initial the square. When all the squares are completed the road to the item is complete.

This path system works as well for an mp3 player as it does for a video game or candy bar. The number of squares and tasks you choose coordinates with the desired item. Just like in real life, more expensive items take more work and more time to achieve.

LITTLE HELPING HANDS

Chore and reward systems can work with children as young as two. While a two-year-old won't be very efficient at vacuuming, there are ways a toddler can contribute to smoother days. (See below.) Starting a reward system and building self-esteem and self-belief at a young age is a great gift to give a child.

Samantha was eighteen months old when I started our first chore and reward system. Using a piece of construction paper, I made twenty one-by-one-inch squares. At the bottom I made one large square and put a picture of an Elmo helium balloon. Each time she cleaned up her toys, was a good listener for the day, got dressed without a fight, went to sleep without a fight, or went to the bathroom "on the potty," I let her choose a sticker to place on a square. (The stickers were all her favorite characters: animals, dinosaurs, Barney, butterflies.)

When all of the squares were stickered, we made a special adventure out of purchasing her balloon from the local grocery store. While I needed several grocery items, I left that list at home so the entire trip could be devoted to Sammy's accomplishment. Sammy took great pride in picking her balloon and brought the reward chart along to proudly explain (as best she could) her journey.

TAKE A STEP FORWARD

Set up a chore and reward system to create smoother days and team unity in your home. Begin marking age-appropriate tasks to delegate. Explain the process to each child and agree on a goal item. Mark a date within the next ten days to have the charts made and begin using your new system.

If you do not have kids in the home: Why not create a reward system for yourself? Choose any home maintenance tasks that have been hard to routinely maintain. Make a checklist and choose a reward for your accomplishment.

TOOLS, RESOURCES, AND REFERENCES
    ☒   View samples of chore and reward systems online.

.

mini-makeover

YOU'VE GOTTA HAVE FRIENDS
Fostering a Positive Support Network

"I get by with a little help from my friends."—*John Lennon*

One of the greatest influences on anyone's quality of life is the people around them. It is impossible to achieve balance without balancing relationships. From friendships, to colleagues, to relatives, this Mini-Makeover takes you step-by-step through "organizing the people in your life." You'll learn who you need to have on your team, how to handle negative people, and how the people in your life affect you.

Step 1: Organizing the People in Your Life

Step 2: The People Principle: How Are You Affected by the People in Your Life?

Step 3: Make a List, Checking it Twice

Step 4: Connecting

Step 5: Here's Looking at You

you've gotta have friends step 1

Organizing the People in Your Life

"A friend is one who walks in when others walk out"—*Walter Winchell*

Spending time with uplifting and encouraging people creates contentment, laughter, and fulfillment. However, if we don't organize and choose who we spend our time with (and how we spend that time), we can find ourselves feeling discontented, anxious, or depressed. In this Step we will look at who we spend our time with and how much time we spend.

GRAB YOUR CALENDAR

Our first task is to inventory all the people we spend time with on a daily, weekly, or monthly basis. Use your calendar, cell phone, and address book to help you remember everyone. Do not include appointments (like dentist, hair, etc.), which are "musts" in life maintenance. Include only people you CHOOSE to see (going to lunch, coffee, volunteer work, stopping by someone's house) and those you feel OBLIGATED to see (your husband's-cousin's-sister's-brother). If you work outside the home, also include co-workers you have lunch with, commute with, or visit with during the day. Make sure to include family members you see at least monthly. Use the worksheet "Organizing Our Relationships," and write people's names in the left-hand column. Write down all of the names before continuing.

Organizing Your Relationships Worksheet

Name	How much time do I spend with him/her each week?	Personality Type	Change to Be Made	Card Communication

HOW MUCH TIME DO YOU SPEND?

Next to each person's name, write down how much time is spent together on a monthly basis; for example, an hour a day, two hours a week, once a month for one hour. Don't worry about being exact—approximations will work just fine.

TAKE A STEP FORWARD

Complete the Organizing Our Relationships worksheet. Although a simple assignment, it is a very important one, affecting overall life quality greatly as explained in the Steps to follow.

TOOLS, RESOURCES, AND REFERENCES

- ☑ Additional copies of the Organizing Our Relationships worksheet are available online.

you've gotta have friends
step 2

THE PEOPLE PRINCIPLE
How Are You Affected by
the People in Your Life?

"Keep away from people who try to belittle your ambitions. Small people always do that, but the really great make you feel that you, too, can become great."—*Mark Twain*

In the last Step we created a list of the people that we are either obligated to see or choose to spend time with. In this Step we evaluate how that time affects our lives. Have you ever spent time with someone who had absolutely nothing positive to say about anything? After an hour of listening to her, how did you feel? What about spending time with someone who is just brimming with life and happiness? How did you feel after an hour of time with her?

Whether we like it or not, we are greatly influenced by those we spend time with, and that influence can be positive or negative. It is true that we do have control over HOW WE REACT to things; however, who wants to spend all their time trying to react positively to negative people? We can't always be doing "cognitive reprogramming." It's much better to make wise choices and spend our time with the people who compliment us. That's doesn't mean that everyone has to be "high on life," but it means that we limit those people who are likely to bring us down. By spending most of our time with positive people, we reserve some energy to positively influence the negative people that we do choose (or have) to be around.

Read through the seven following categories and assign each person on your list the category most representative of how the person affects you. Write this number in the Personality Type column. If someone ranks in more than one category, you can list both categories under their personality column rating. And yes, family members fall into these categories too!

1. Perfectly Pleasant Patty: These are the people whom you love to spend time with. The time is healthy, upbeat, inspiring. You wish you could spend more time together. You leave your meetings feeling very invigorated and good about yourself and the world.

2. 20/80 Katy: These are people whom, for the most part, you enjoy. They are fun, encouraging and appreciate you for who you are and encourage you in what you are trying to achieve — most of the time. There is an occasional bump in the road, a bit of negativity here and there, and perhaps a tad of gossip, but no one is perfect!

3. 50–50 Kind of Nifty Nelly: These people are caught between the glass being half-empty and half-full. They tend to be positive half of the time, but counteract that positiveness with negativity the other half of the time.

4. Sinking Sally: Sinking Sally is on a ship that is slowly going down due to negative thinking and choosing immobility over action. Although she would like to think she is on the path to change, she is a lot of "talk" and very little "walk." This type of person often seeks your advice (sometimes over and over again about the same problem) but never takes positive action. She is more interested in pondering change than creating a positive life.

5. Gossip Gloria: Gloria won't be changing her life any time soon. In fact, why should she, since she lives vicariously through everyone around her and has plenty of ideas on how to change their lives? (She'll share those ideas with you, whether you want to hear them or not.) Can you say, Gossip Gloria = bad news?

6. Surface Sarah: Sarah seems positive on the surface; she may even be an outstanding citizen or churchgoer. But when you

get to know Surface Sarah, you will find that although she talks a good talk, she often seems bitter or jealous, or has rude things to say about others. Surface Sarah can seem so wonderful and generous on the outside, it can be hard to realize what lurks beneath that shiny exterior.

7. Controlling Carla: Carla knows exactly how you should live your life and she is going to tell you. She is possessive, controlling, and downright bossy.

TAKE A STEP FORWARD

From the seven categories, fill in the category name that best describes each person on your list. Make sure you have all of the people you spend time with on your worksheet along with their categories before moving on to the next Step.

you've gotta have friends step 3

Making a List, Checking It Twice

"A friend is a gift you give yourself."—*Robert Louis Stevenson*

You should now have a list of the people you spend time with and an assessment of how that time affects you. In this Step we examine what changes would help you achieve balance and rewarding relationships, and we'll make some plans to take action.

1. Do you have at least one Perfectly Pleasant Patty?

   IF YES: Do you see this person at least once a week (or talk with them on the phone)? If yes, GOOD—keep it up. We all need a Perfectly Pleasant Patty to help lift our spirits, inspire us, and engage us, at least weekly. If the person you have on your list does not have that much time (you won't know until you ask—and even a five-minute call will do sometimes) then you need to go hunt down another Perfectly Pleasant Patty. I encourage you to spend at least sixty minutes each week with this type of personality (more if you can).

   IF NO: Then it is time to be on the lookout for one. Consider the networking opportunities in the MTM Online or looking up a MTM-Mini Group in your area. Since we are all engaged in this challenge because we are looking for positive change, my guess is that there are quite a few inspirational and fun women reading this book. Spending time emailing or talking on the phone is just as effective as spending time together in person. I encourage you to spend at least sixty minutes each week with this type of personality (more if you can).

In the CHANGE TO BE MADE column of the Organizing Your Relationships Worksheet, write down what you need to do. Do you need to keep doing what you're doing? Find another (or a first) Perfectly Pleasant Patty?

2. How many 20/80 Katys do you have?

    These are the most common long-lasting friendships. They weather the ups and downs of life and remain mostly encouraging and positive. Sometimes when we get busy with life, we forget to really keep in touch with the 20/80 Katys. Days go by and before we know it, it has been weeks or even months since we have spoken. The 20/80 Katys are very valuable foundations for our lives. Have you been spending time each week or every other week with your foundation friends? If not, how can you change that? Record it in the CHANGE TO BE MADE column (and of course, write down on your calendar when you plan to implement that change).

3. How many 50–50 Kind of Nifty Nellies do you have in your life?

    Think of these people as "break-evens." They might enrich your life some, but for the ways they enrich it, they also counterbalance with negativity. To be quite blunt here, these people simply take up your one nonrenewable resource—time. They do not move you forward, but at least they don't drag you backward. You should certainly try to spend less time with these people and more time with the Katys and Pattys. How could you do that? Record your thoughts in the CHANGE TO BE MADE column.

4. Are you trying to save a Sinking Sally?

    As women, we often feel the need to nurture and rescue. I have tried to save many a Sinking Sally. On the upside, it often worked. On the downside, it can be quite overwhelming. Of course, we make the world a better place when we take someone who wants to change (but may need an extra push here and there) and help them. I believe that is important. However, I have learned the hard way that we can't try to save a bunch of people at once, or we will deplete our own energy and end up becoming a Sinking Sally ourselves. Try to limit the Sinking Sallys in your life to one at a time. If you need to make any changes in this category, record it in the CHANGE TO BE MADE column.

5. **Cutting Loose the Controlling Carlas and Gossip Glorias**
    You can probably guess what I am going to say here: WHY ARE YOU SPENDING TIME WITH THEM? There is no benefit for your life here. These people sap your joy and your energy. Write three simple words in the CHANGE TO BE MADE column: cut them loose.

6. **Have you uncovered a Surface Sarah?**
    It can take a while to see the "other side" of a Surface Sarah. In fact, you may have become so close by the time you see the other side that you find it hard to believe that it could really be her. Surface Sarahs are master manipulators. Learn to exit out of awkward conversations quickly. If after a month you don't see improvements, say so long to Surface Sarahs.

Note: You likely have noticed that I am more adamant about how to handle certain personality types than in other areas of the challenge. This is because spending time with the wrong people (or talking to them for that matter) is the single-most influential outside force in my life. The Surface Sarahs, Gossip Glorias, and Controlling Carlas DO NOT WANT TO CHANGE but they do WANT TO CHANGE YOU — and it's not for the better! This doesn't mean you need to ex-communicate them completely, but you do need to severely limit your exposure if you truly want to lead a healthy life.

HANDLING OBLIGATIONS

Now, some of these people you may be OBLIGATED to see. For example, your in-laws may be Sinking Sallys, but if you plan on making your marriage work, you must adapt and live with it. However, before you commit to spending time together, make sure it is a true obligation. Sometimes we think we "should" or "ought" to do something—when in reality that expectation is from an outdated belief system. If it is a true obligation, ask yourself: can it be minimized? For example, if you see your in-laws every other week for a three-hour dinner, could you change that to a once-a-month dinner? Or could you change the dinners from three hours to two? Doing so may not be easy, and you may catch "a bit of flack," but that is short-term. You will be creating a long-term change that is much healthier for you—and thus much healthier for your immediate family.

TAKE A STEP FORWARD

Analyze your findings and record the changes that need to be made in the CHANGE TO BE MADE column. If you are spending most of your time with unhealthy or toxic people, look at how you can free up that time for the people that bring positive energy and inspiration to your life. Choose two changes from the CHANGE TO BE MADE column and add them to the Active Task List in your CAN. Add the remaining tasks to your Short-Term Task List.

you've gotta have friends
step 4

Connecting

"The walls we build around us to keep out the sadness also keep out the joy."—*Jim Rohn*

Take a look at the Prioritizing Relationships worksheet and its three columns:

A. People I need to communicate with more (email, phone, or in-person)
B. People that are just fine and should remain status quo
C. People I need to spend less time with

Prioritizing Relationships		
The A List	The B List	The C List
People I need to spend more time with	People who are fine as they are—remain "status quo"	People I need to spend less time with

Transfer each name from the Organizing Your Relationships worksheet to one of these columns based on your findings in the last Step.

TAKE A STEP FORWARD

This Step has two parts. First, grab the phone. Skim down the first column, where you have listed those people you need to communicate with more. Call one and let her know you are thinking about her. Call another person from this list (or ask the first person you called) if she can get together within the next thirty days. Set a date. Voila—part one done. (Don't let me stop you though—keep on moving down the list if you're game. The more time you spend with the people in column A, the more joy and contentment you will find.)

On the Organizing Your Relationships worksheet, jot down the date and person called in the Card/Communication column. This will help you remember with whom you still need to connect and also help monitor how much time goes by between communications.

Part two of this Step involves a fun-filled field trip. Grab your checkbook, grab your list, and head to the card store. Purchase a collection of cards to keep handy. Consider putting a few in your purse so you can write messages when you have unexpected time, like waiting at an appointment.

A handwritten note brightens the day of the recipient, especially in today's world where most everything is done via email. Find an hour or two to enjoy browsing card shops and choosing cards. This week, send out at least three handwritten cards to people on the A-list. From here on out, carry several note cards with a pen in your purse (tuck in a plastic bag to protect) or To-Read envelope and write cards when you are waiting for an appointment or have time to spare.

If you are the creative type, consider visiting a crafting super-store, rubber stamp store, or scrapbooking store instead of a card store and purchasing supplies to make your own cards. Or opt for a combination and intersperse homemade with store-bought cards.

Make a note of cards sent on the Organizing Your Relationships worksheet. Add these lists behind the Contacts and Connections tab of your Headquarters. Use the Contacts and Connects tab as an address book in order to make connecting easier.

TOOLS, RESOURCES, AND REFERENCES

- ☑ Additional copies of the Organizing Your Relationships and Prioritizing Relationships worksheet are available online.
- ☑ While nothing can match the personal touch of a handwritten note, there are some very creative ecards available! Stop online to view my list of favorites.
- ☒ Printable address book pages are available in the printable area.

you've gotta have friends
step 5

Here's Looking at You

"Our outward life is a mirror of what we feel and believe inside."—
Brook Noel

Throughout this Mini-Makeover we have examined the people in
our lives and how spending time together affects us. It is just as
important to assess how we affect others.

Review the personality type descriptions. Imagine a friend was
listing your name on their worksheet. How do you think she would
categorize you? What category would you like to be in? Record
your thoughts in your journal.

As in most life areas, like attracts like. If you gossip a lot, you're
likely going to find a plethora of Gossip Glorias at your beck and
call. If you are a 20/80 Katy, don't be surprised if your list has
mostly these personality types. Our lives are reflections of what we
feel and believe inside.

TAKE A STEP FORWARD

Consider how you answered the questions in this Step. If how you
believe you would be categorized and how you would like to be
categorized is different, what steps can you take to bridge the gap?
Identify one small change in your journal and then begin implementing it today.

mini-makeover

Joy and Purpose-Filled Living

We must not, in trying to think about how we can make a big difference, ignore the small daily differences we can make which, over time, add up to big differences that we often cannot foresee."—*Marian Wright Edelman*

Have you ever felt there must be "something more" but been unable to identify what it is? Have you ever felt your life is a series of "to-dos" but that you aren't really living? These feelings are often caused by a disconnection between actions and values. This Mini-Makeover will help you rediscover passion, values, purpose and joy in your life.

Step 1: Values—Our Lens to View the World

Step 2: Giving Back

Step 3: Where Are You Going? Discover and Write Your Life Story

Step 4: Create a Vision Statement

Step 5: The Art of the Invisible Blessing

joy and purpose step 1

Values—Our Lens to View the World

"The highest courage is to dare to be yourself in the face of adversity. Choosing right over wrong, ethics over convenience, and truth over popularity...these are the choices that measure your life. Travel the path of integrity without looking back, for there is never a wrong time to do the right thing." —*Unknown*

I was delivering a keynote to a group of mental-health professionals at their annual conference when I asked, "How many people here can stand up, right now, and tell me the three values that govern your life?" Out of 300 attendees only two hands were raised. Even I was surprised at the result—especially given the audience. Without clear and guiding values it is hard to live a life of purpose.

The afternoons of our annual CYLC Orlando workshop are spent building Personal Power Decks and exploring values, affirmations, and other life-guiding tools. When we started the value exercise, I asked if anyone could define the word value. Women struggled. I struggled too. I could "feel" what a value was, but I could not find a sentence to express my thoughts. My daughter, who had joined us for the activity, raised her hand. "A value is something you stay true to." I smiled, thanked her, and said, "Exactly."

Clear values act as a filter. In times of indecision, we can compare options to our guiding values to make a decision. Values are the seams which shape the fabric of our lives. Without defined values, we have torn seams where the unwanted can sneak in, and our energy can sneak out. Values allow us to advance confidently in a meaningful direction. Without them we will be blown around by the emotions, people, and external events of the day.

Below is a list of values. Read each word carefully. Choose three to five words that resonate as values you long to "stay true to." Many people find it easier to reduce the list by crossing off nonpriority values and continuing to reduce the list until three to five values are left.

There is not a right or wrong answer. Do not concern yourself with the messages of others and what "should be important." Try on each of the values. Choose values that matter to you and provide light for this stage of your life journey. Transfer those that resonate most into your journal.

TAKE A STEP FORWARD

While many of these words carry similar meanings, certain words will resonate with you more than others. Begin by crossing off values that are certainly not among your top five. Then take a break and come back to the list in a half hour or so. Try to cross off at least half of the remaining items. Continue working in this fashion until a clear list of three to five values emerges. Write each value on an index card for your Personal Power Deck. On the back of the card, list ways you can live this value. The three to five values you choose will be needed for the Vision Statement Step in this section.

Values

Accomplishment	Family	Pleasure
Accountability	Freedom	Positive attitude
Accuracy	Friendship	Power
Adventure	Fun	Practicality
Beauty	Goodness	Preservation
Calm, peace	Gratitude	Privacy
Challenge	Hard work	Progress
Change	Harmony	Security
Cleanliness, orderliness	Honesty	Self-reliance
Commitment	Honor	Service
Communication	Independence	Simplicity
Community	Innovation	Stability
Continuous improvement	Integrity	Strength
Cooperation	Justice	Timeliness
Creativity	Knowledge	Tradition
Democracy	Leadership	Tranquility
Discipline	Love, Romance	Truth
Discovery	Loyalty	Unity
Excellence	Meaning	Variety
Fairness	Money	Wisdom
Faith	Personal Growth	

This is only a small list of values. You can add your own values or search online for "value list" to go more in depth.

TOOLS, RESOURCES, AND REFERENCES
☒ View the full list of three hundred values online and work through step-by-step exercises to hone in on your core values.

joy and purpose step 2

Giving Back

"I always had a dream that when I am asked to give an accounting of my life to a higher court, it will be like this: so, empty your pockets. What have you got left of your life? Any dreams that were unfilled? Any unused talent we gave you when you were born that you have left? Any unsaid compliments or bits of love that you haven't spread around? And I will answer, 'I have nothing to return. I spent everything you gave me. I'm as naked as the day I was born.'"—*Erma Bombeck*

As I built this challenge, I spent a great deal of time analyzing at which points in my life I felt the most complete. Not that I am incomplete, but you know the times I speak of, those times when you are "in the zone," or more balanced than at other times. As I recalled my most harmonic times, I looked for common denominators.

During my periods of contentment, I was heavily involved in volunteer efforts of some kind. I have helped out with different student organizations such as Girl Scouts and 4-H. I have created and coordinated plays for youth groups. My mom tells a story when at age ten I put on a bake sale and sold $300 worth of cookies so I could send the money to help repair the Statue of Liberty. (My arm grew tired after mixing one batch of cookie dough, so my mom helped with the rest. Perhaps that is why her memory of this event is so vivid.)

A few Christmases back, I noticed that I experienced the "holiday blues" in a more pronounced way than previous years. The holidays had come upon me so quickly and then in a flash they were gone. When I looked for the source of my sadness, I realized that I had been so busy with work endeavors that year that I had not engaged in leading any gift or food roundup programs or played "Secret Santa" to a needy family.

The greatest gift we can ever give is our self. It is a gift no one else can duplicate. Whether it's weekly, monthly, quarterly, or yearly, giving of ourselves connects us to the world around us.

TAKE A STEP FORWARD

What part of your self are you giving back to the world? Does this add joy to your life or do you need to rethink your outreach? If you are not currently reaching out in service, what opportunities might exist to enrich your life and the lives of others? Choose a cause where you would like to contribute your energies. Use the Personal Quota from Step 11 of the Toolbox to guide you in selecting a time and vehicle for outreach that aligns with your time.

TOOLS, RESOURCES, AND REFERENCES

☑ Looking for ideas on how to give back? From overseas care packages to local volunteer opportunities, our comprehensive online guide provides quick links to a variety of worthwhile endeavors seeking support.

joy and purpose step 3

WHERE ARE YOU GOING?
Discover and Write Your Life Story

"The pen that creates our life story rests in our own hand."—*Brook Noel*

Although I write mostly nonfiction, I write fiction and short stories for fun. What I like most about writing fiction is the ability to rewrite, rework, change a word, swap out a chapter, or modify an entire plotline. One small change can create a completely different ending.

Even though our lives are not fiction, one small change can also create a completely different day, week, month, year, or life. Sometimes we forget that the pen that creates our life story rests in our own hand.

I have been doing a lot of speaking at groups, expos, and conventions these past months. Hundreds of women have embraced the concept of the *Challenge* and started implementing the positive steps in their lives. Yet, for every woman who starts the program, there are likely women who never will. There are also women who will start the program and stop. There are other women who think change at this stage in their life is impossible.

I have seen this program change the lives of countless women. I have excitedly watched women transform into the whole, centered, and happy people they have longed to be. More than once I have wondered: *Why do some people believe change is not possible? How do we forget that the only place change can begin is right here, right now? How do we quit accepting the cards life deals and instead challenge life to the fullest? And when we get off track in our thinking, as we all will from time to time, how do we quickly return to our positive and affirming ways?*

The answers to these questions are not simple, but multifaceted and complex. However, I do believe the first place to explore is our past. I have seen women let the past create their future.

Because we have lived a certain way, or been expected to "be" a certain way, we give someone else the pen to write our story and we just turn the pages. As long as we are on this earth we have the power to *choose*. We can choose to take back our pen and write our story, or we can choose to leave it in the hands of others.

If you are very, very, very hungry, so hungry your stomach is growling incessantly while you sit in the living room, what would you do? Odds are you would choose to eat to satiate this hunger. In that one moment (and hundreds of others throughout the day), you *choose* to make a change in your life. You *choose* to feed that hunger. What would happen if you chose not to have a snack or meal? The growling would not stop. You would become hungrier and hungrier and emptier and emptier.

Each day we can choose to feed or starve our dreams, our soul, our happiness, our purpose, and our relationships. Are you choosing to feed your soul? Or are you waiting for someone or something else to feed you?

Just as you can choose to get out of bed or go to bed, eat or not eat, you can also choose to be happy. You can choose to take a step forward. You can choose to make today matter. You can write your own life story.

TAKE A STEP FORWARD

Pay attention to the choices you make today. Consider the impact of each choice and how it affects your story. Journal about who you have given the "pen" over to in your life. What steps do you need to take to begin writing the story of your life? What is one step you can take within the next hour? Write that step down, and then *choose* to take that step now.

joy and purpose step

Create a Vision Statement

"One day Alice came to a fork in the road and saw a Cheshire cat in a tree. 'Which road do I take?' she asked. 'Where do you want to go?' was his response. 'I don't know,' Alice answered. 'Then,' said the cat, 'it doesn't matter.'"—*Alice in Wonderland*

If I asked you to abandon all of your daily commitments for a one-week period in order to drive from Los Angeles to New York, I bet the first question you would have is: "Why?"

I reply with, "Because I want you to." How is that for great motivation? Unless you are my husband, I would imagine that doesn't really spark any desire in you.

Let's try this again. I ask you to drive from Los Angeles to New York. "Why?" you ask. "Because there is two million dollars waiting for me and I am willing to give you half if you go pick it up." After clarifying the money is legal and there is no danger, would you be more motivated to consider my request? For many of us, that might tip the scale and put our foot on the accelerator. (I am not implying money is the only, or best, motivator. Many people with mounds of money are miserable.)

Besides two million dollars, what changed between the first and second request? The first request is purposeless; the second request provides a clear and concise vision and purpose for the journey.

Everything worthwhile begins with a vision. Think of a vision as the "big picture" of why you make specific choices and take certain actions. A vision statement is a guiding light which allows us to live each day with purpose and clarity.

Vision statements and goals are very different. Goals are self-encompassed measures to move a person from point A to point B. A vision is the overall "theme" we want to live in our life (or at least in this season of our life). Our working goals become the ladder to that vision. Without a vision, you are likely to wander aimlessly, moving from goal to goal or abandoning goals altogether because there is no uniting purpose tying goals to vision. *A clear vision statement will help us choose goals that are right for us. There may be a million things we want to do — but only a few that we actually need to do.*

Let's use an excerpt from my vision statement to see how a vision statement can guide goals and choices.

Excerpt of Brook's Vision Statement:

To live a compassionate, gratitude-filled life and use my creativity to help women overcome their challenges.

With this vision statement, what would you advise if I told you I was thinking about attending law school? You would not need to be a life coach to advise that is not a great choice for advancing my vision.

A clear vision allows us to choose compatible goals and daily actions.

A vision statement is not a dusty document shoved in a drawer, but an active, living purpose to revisit each day to clarify daily goals, actions, and decisions. Used daily, a vision statement anchors us in our purpose; we accept responsibilities and tasks that are in alignment, and reject activities not in alignment.

HERE ARE SOME MISSION STATEMENT EXAMPLES FROM READERS

"My ultimate purpose is to have the best, harmonious life possible…to enjoy my kids, to enjoy my home, to enjoy my husband, to enjoy life — not later but NOW."

"My life will be an extension of my soul — seeking truth, beauty, and simplicity in every moment."

"Each day I will greet God and take his hand to create joy, harmony, and peace in the lives of all I touch. I will avoid the negative traps of life and look to the positive and possible at every turn."

TAKE A STEP FORWARD

Gather the list of values identified in the first Step of this section. Use these values as the foundation for your vision statement. My example includes the values of compassion, gratitude, creativity, and rising above challenges. It will likely take more than a few tries to create a vision statement that feels inherently "good" to you. In your journal, write down sentences that incorporate your value words. Keep moving the words around and experimenting with sentence structure until you arrive at one to two sentences you are comfortable with.

Once you have your vision statement, type or nicely write out several copies on index cards. Add one to the inside cover of your CAN to help keep you "on purpose." Place the others where you will see them often. Memorize this statement. Recite it daily. When you are faced with a decision and are unsure which way to turn, consult your vision statement. Does the option at hand support or detract from your purpose? Let the statement guide your final decision.

TOOLS, RESOURCES, AND REFERENCES

☒   View sample vision statements online and learn how to create a vision statement portrait to serve as an attractive visual prompt.

joy and purpose step 5

The Art of the Invisible Blessing

"You cannot live a perfect day without doing something for someone who will never be able to repay you." —*John Wooden*

To give is a wonderful thing; to give completely anonymously is even more wonderful. Without the need for a "thank you" or a pat on the back, our giving is focused completely on the recipient versus an affirmation of ourselves. Giving through an "invisible blessing" is the most powerful gift of all. This simple story shares a memory of a woman who had truly mastered the "invisible blessing."

THE WOMAN AND THE POSTMAN

Once again, the tiny, rural Post Office in our Northwoods Wisconsin town had been properly notified. The "Postmaster," simply known as John, had received his yearly letter (addressed to "John, Post Office" —first name only, no street and number, no zip code) asking him to select five little girls "from Santa's List" who would love to receive a Christmas doll. Now, John knew everything and everybody—if you wanted to find out something, or get the local "scuttlebutt" you went to John—so he set about checking his postal routes, making his recommendations, and had the season's list secretly delivered to the woman.

From about November 1st on, the woman's dining room table became covered with snippets of lace and ribbons, buttons and bows, velvets and satins, along with the five Madame Alexander dolls that had been ordered for that year through the mail.

Her needles and thread in hand, and an old Singer sewing machine by her side, the woman began to weave her yearly Christmas magic. Party clothes, sportswear, ball gowns, warm winter coats, she fashioned them all, until each doll had a wardrobe beyond any girl's dreams.

A week before Christmas, she had the dolls delivered to the stoop of the Post Office, beautifully wrapped and tagged for each child with a note from Santa. John would notify the families that a special package had arrived and needed to be picked up before he closed on Christmas Eve.

The week after Christmas, John would usually receive a thank you note, or two, or three, which needed to be delivered in return. Sworn to secrecy he would pass on the child-scribbled notes to "whom it may concern."

Then one fall a funeral came to pass, November came and went, and the list hadn't been asked for, the Christmas dolls didn't arrive, and the magic faded. Not long after that John put in for retirement. The Post Office became renovated with zip codes + 4, an automated sorter, updated routing and regulations, and rules too numerous to count or accept; a new post man was "brought up from the city" — all in the name of "progress." Still bound by his oath of secrecy, John's knowledge about the woman and the dolls retired with him.

EPILOGUE

Every year when we went to my Aunt's for Thanksgiving dinner, I'd notice her table had just been cleared of a sewing project. She would set a fine table and our family would eat and feast until we could barely eat any more. And then, over her delicious pumpkin pie, my talk would turn to speculation about the mystery dolls that would surely arrive (just like mine had) at the Post Office — just in time for Christmas. My Aunt Joan would just give me a wink and her yearly reply, "Surely, my dear, you'll have another piece of pie…"

TAKE A STEP FORWARD

In the hustle and bustle of daily living it is common to feel life is about accomplishment or maintaining status quo. A joy-filled life is built on relationships, connections, love, gratitude, kindness, and caring. Create a ritual of invisibly blessing someone. It can be an extravagant ritual done once a year, or a simple practice done weekly.

mini-makeover

The Worn-Out Woman

Feel like you are stuck in a rut or worn-out? Perhaps all you need is an "Attitude Makeover." In this Mini-Makeover you'll learn easy-to-implement self-coaching strategies to actively take control of your thoughts and make changes that will help you achieve greater happiness, joy, and contentment.

Step 1: Ask for Help

Step 2: The Invisible Coach

Step 3: Self-Coaching

Step 4: Fighting Back Fatigue

Step 5: Creating Personal Power Scripts

the worn-out woman
step 1

Ask for Help

"There will always be times when you feel discouraged.
I too, have felt despair many times in my life,
but I do not keep a chair for it; I will not entertain it.
It is not allowed to eat from my plate."
—*Clarissa Pinkola Estes*

We are not Super Woman…she had a cape, and we already gave ours up. Most superheroes even have sidekicks: Batman has Robin, Superman can count on Lois Lane, and Luke Skywalker has Yoda and Obi-Wan. While trying to attain superhero status might make us look independent or strong, it is only an illusion.

How many people in this world operate completely independently, capable of "doing it all" on their own? I cannot think of one successful CEO who is not backed by talented executives. I am unaware of a single politician that isn't helped by aides or campaign managers. Schools and churches have boards for guidance.

Instead of striving to "do it all" or beating yourself up when you cannot tackle everything solo, try on a team mentality. Find supportive players to be a part of your team and ask for help when you need it. Doing everything ourselves does not makes us stronger, it makes us lonelier and needlessly stressed.

TAKE A STEP FORWARD

How have you tried to "do it all" in your life? What were the results? Who can be a part of your support team? Who can you ask for help? Take your journal and spend half an hour brainstorming a list of areas you could use help with. Each week ask for help on at last three things. When asked with kindness and sincerity, many people are willing to help. The helper feels valued and respected when asked for advice or assistance. Never assume people will not help you—ask.

worn-out woman step 2

The Invisible Coach

"Whether you think you can or think you can't, you're right."—*Eleanor Roosevelt*

Remember those cartoons where a character has a small angel on one shoulder and a devil on the other? The character is trying to make a decision and both are whispering input into an ear. Have you ever noticed a little voice in your own head? Kind of like a built-in coach, except this voice rarely says anything positive. Instead she whispers phrases like: *what were you thinking? You should have known better. Don't even bother trying. I knew this wouldn't work. You never see things through.* This voice belongs to your default coach—the Internal Critic.

Everyone has a Critic-Coach. When you see someone with a great attitude, you can bet they have learned this Critic exists, and have also learned how to "duct tape" her quiet!

We are not born with a Critic. We start life full of hope, wonder, and expectation. When we are little, we do not give up just because something does not go our way. We do not belittle ourselves. Instead we try even harder. You can see this in a youngster who is learning to walk. When he falls, he doesn't choose to spend the balance of his life crawling around. Instead, he tries again, and again, and again. If an infant is hungry, she does not scream or cry once and give up if food does not arrive. She will continue to make herself heard until she is fed. Toddlers do not greet the day weighed down with past regrets or future worries. Instead, each day is a fresh canvas, ready for exploration.

In late 2006 my then eleven-year-old daughter and I were about to sit down and make our goal posters for the year ahead. I was digging around for a long-lost collage paper and so intently focused on the hunt I was distracted from our conversation. I knew I must have said something problematic when Sammy shrilled, "MOM!"

I stood up straight and tried to remember the last words I had spoken. I didn't have much time to wonder before Sammy continued with a startled reprimand.

"MOTHER! You almost doubted yourself! Say you're sorry to yourself! Say you're sorry to your brain!"

The context of the conversation came back. We were talking about a trip we wanted to take and I began a statement with "Well, if I...." At that moment Sammy cut me off. In our house words like "if" and "try" are not used. We use empowering and affirmative words. We commit. We expect the best. We are not perfectionists and we are not disappointed in ourselves when we "miss the mark," but we enter each day believing "we can and we will," instead of "I might and I'll try."

Think about the word "try." What type of confidence does the word "try" exude? A while back I learned I had gallstones, and my doctor suggested my gall bladder be removed. I had many questions and scheduled an appointment with the specialist. The information he provided helped me realize having the surgery was in my best interest. However, if he had told me, "Well, I am trying to take out your gall bladder, and if I can we should see some relief in your pain," I would have left his office. Try does not exude faith, competence, or commitment. Words like "try" and "if" are escape routes for living.

I have been asked, "Isn't it better to try than not do anything?" I do not believe you need to use the word "try." When my daughter wanted to learn to ride her bike, she didn't say, "I am going to try to learn to ride my bike today." Instead she said, "I'm learning to ride my bike today." Little words carry big connotations; "try" isn't an action—it is a precursor to action.

My daughter was shocked when I used the word "if." Her shock affirmed that this must have been one of the few times a nonaffirming statement came from my mouth. I have seen her before in my workplace, replacing the "ifs" of employees and it always fills me with pride. This isn't a steadfast rule that I enforced in our home, but a quality I wanted to exemplify and in turn hoped she would inherit. Not only did she inherit it, she internalized it, and has basically become the "Positive Patrol."

Interestingly, we aren't all born with "ifs." When we are little we don't say, "When I grow up, if I can be President..." Instead, if asked, "What will you be when you grow up?" we announce proudly, "I will be President." At a young age maybe we have not considered all the obstacles or barriers. Maybe we do not even know what an obstacle is; regardless we do know what "belief" is and we have it down to our toes. So where does it go? When do the "whens" turn to "ifs"?

WHEN DO THE "WHENS" TURN TO "IFS?"

Why do we find children so inspirational? Part of it is their innocence but there is much more. The magic within a child lies largely in the fact they are untarnished by worry, blame, guilt, and the stress of adult life. When we are around children we remember how to "believe."

Yet somewhere in our young lives, things begin to change. Our aspirations, dreams, and ideas are criticized. When we paint a pink tree and purple sky and an authority figure corrects us—letting us know that trees are not pink and skies are not purple—the little creative voice becomes quieter. After enough of this feedback, we learn to be a critic to ourselves. We learn to second-guess our dreams, doubt our approach, and belittle our efforts. We develop this internal critic that follows us everywhere, and her main ammunition is negativity and guilt. Our internal critic does not believe in much of anything: if she did, she would cease to exist.

Eventually we become adults. We often feel a push and pull in our lives. We go from high to low and back again. We bounce between feeling empowered and feeling empty. It becomes easy to see why when you think about having two different messages in your mind. That childlike mind encouraging you to take risks, become more, live more, dream more, and then the critic who is reprimanding you for silly ideas, bad odds, and wasted time.

Imagine a woman getting out of bed in the morning, ready to create a positive change and have a wonderful attitude. Standing right behind her is another woman who keeps whispering critical comments in her ear: *You know you can't do it. Haven't you failed at this before? I am sure this won't last a whole week.*

If you were to see such a thing, what would be the first suggestion you would make to the woman seeking to change her attitude? I would tell her to ditch that critic. It is obvious in this example because we can visualize two separate people with two separate voices. It is not this obvious in our own lives, because the critic is internal. Yet, our predicament is the same as the aforementioned woman. We desire a positive life and attitude, while our critical programming bombards us at every turn.

HAVING HER SAY

Stop and pause today to think about your own internal critic. Has your critic surfaced at all yet in this *Challenge*? Did she tell you: *You are behind. You won't see this program through. You know you can't finish. You didn't do the exercise right.* In your journal write down any ways she has surfaced.

In the next paragraph we are going to begin silencing the critic. Doing so is easier when we let her have her say. Take a page in your journal and let her speak. Let her write a letter with all of her bad advice, negativity, and criticisms. Give her one full page, nothing more and nothing less. As soon as the page is filled, immediately continue reading. (Don't stop here and let the critic linger.)

QUIETING THE CRITIC

Can we find a place where these extreme opposites—critic and child—can both survive? How long can fire and ice coexist? Not for long. One characteristic will have to dominate. Unfortunately it is often the critic, because she is louder, obnoxious, and she has undermined you for so long, that you may have begun to undermine yourself. The "good days" are the days where something prompts you back to that childlike state of seeing the good in everything, finding wonder in the simple, and magic in the moment. The bad days are the days the critic speaks so loudly that the child hides.

What do we do with this critic we didn't invite and certainly don't want to entertain? We isolate her and we isolate her behavior. We learn to speak up, grow stronger, and we refuse to let her, or her attitude, sit at our table. And we do that through vigilance. We quit listening to her and when we quit, she starves because she needs worry, guilt, and insecurity to survive.

In order to "battle back" we have to start listening to ourselves, both the words we say and the thoughts we think. When we find ourselves thinking in a self-critical way, we shout as loud as my daughter did. Then we apologize to ourselves (and our brain, as Sammy says) and we put a positive message in the place of the negative.

OTHER IDEAS FOR DEALING WITH THE CRITIC

AWARENESS

Because we have been critical of ourselves for so long, we may not realize when we act critically. Become aware of your words. Listen for critical prompts like should, you always, you never, you can't, and if. When I did this awareness work, I wore a rubber band on my wrist. Each time I noticed self-critical thoughts, I snapped it as a reminder to "snap out of it," and replace my thinking with a positive statement. (My wrist really encouraged me to change my thinking quickly!)

GET LOUD

Since we are trying to embrace some of our lost childhood qualities, often acting like a child is the quickest way to do so! What does a child do when she wants to be heard and a group of people are talking and not paying attention? SHE GETS LOUDER. Instead of reasoning with your Critic, make your self-affirming voice louder. Go do something that makes you feel good. Sing and dance. Write a list of fifty things that are great about you, and then say them aloud each time the Critic shows up. Call the Critic names and stick your tongue out. Once your Internal Critic realizes that you are no longer going to let her existence go unchallenged, she will begin to quiet down.

BE SMARTER THAN YOUR CRITIC

Remember that your Critic relies on negativity, guilt, and doubt to survive. Recognize which emotions your Critic relies on. Create a "battle plan" to move past that internal voice.

RE-PARENT YOURSELF

Imagine one of your own children, or a child you care for, has failed a test that she intensely studied for. What would you tell this child? Would you tell the child any of these things?

- I knew you were going to fail.
- I can't believe you thought you would pass the test in the first place.
- You don't work hard enough.
- I wouldn't even bother going back to class, after that score.
- I never thought you were that smart.
- You didn't deserve to pass like the other kids did.
- It'll never get any easier.
- You think that test was bad, wait until you hit high school.

Even though we would not say these things to a child (or anyone for that matter), our mind is often giving this type of message to ourselves when we aren't pleased with where we are at or what we have done. This creates low self-esteem, anxiety, depression, sadness, and loneliness. When you hear the Critic pipe up with discouraging advice, write it down. Then "write back" with the type of statements you would use to encourage a friend or child.

TAKE A STEP FORWARD

Look at the letter with the words of your Critic. On the next page in your journal, write back. Fill your letter with strong and affirmative self-statements. Talk back to your critic concisely and clearly, letting her know you are in control.

the worn-out woman step 3

Self-Coaching Strategies

"Life isn't about finding yourself—life is about creating yourself."—*George Bernard Shaw*

In Make Today Matter Step 10: Self-Belief and Self-Sabotage, we examined the need to treat ourselves as well as we would a close friend. When we are worn-out, often we have become our own worst enemy, treating ourselves with negative words, thoughts, and actions. I find it fascinating we won't treat another human being as we often treat ourselves.

Self-Coaching is the process of emulating the practices of close and supportive friends in our own lives. No one will ever spend as much time in our minds as we will. No one will ever spend as much time with us as we will. Therefore the first key to developing a positive self-esteem is learning how to encourage versus criticize our selves day-in and day-out. However, most of us who need to work on attitude or self-esteem (often intertwined) are far from our own close friend. More often than not, we carry the traits we found on the "enemy" list of Step 10, belittling our accomplishments, criticizing our thinking, and overemphasizing all our shortcomings. We focus on what we left behind instead of what lies ahead and on what we didn't do instead of what we did.

When we begin our self-work, we need to learn to coach ourselves with the supportive attributes of a close friend. Certainly therapy and group work has its place, but for long lasting esteem restructuring we need to learn to be there for ourselves. We aren't going to be with a group or therapist twenty-four hours a day. We are always going to be with our own thoughts. If we work in a group setting one to two hours a week, and then live another 166 hours outside of that supportive environment with our thoughts getting the best of us, we destroy progress as quickly as we build it.

Self-Coaching is not complicated and does not require a coaching degree. The only tool required is a mindfulness of your thoughts and a commitment to take stock of your thoughts. Let's take a look at the typical roles of a team coach.

Is a coach expected to show up for each practice, or do they just show up when it is convenient or they are in the mood? A coach has to be consistent and dedicated to the purpose of his team. Like a coach, we need to "show up" and be ready to manage our thoughts consistently and with dedication.

When a player doesn't perform well, even though they practiced hard, does the coach ignore the performance or belittle the player? A good coach does assess the performance, but they do so while building up the player, versus belittling the player. When we make a mistake or fall short of a goal, we need to evaluate our performance, and analyze how to positively move forward without belittling ourselves. I'll borrow the words of Vince Lombardi, one of the most successful coaches of all time: "It's easy to have faith in yourself and have discipline when you're a winner, when you're number one. What you've got to have is faith and discipline when you're not yet a winner."

Does a coach go to a competition expecting to lose? Of course not; why go or try if losing is the goal? The quickest way to lose is to do nothing. Vince Lombardi said, "Perfection is not attainable. But if we chase perfection, we can catch excellence."

Does a coach change teams if his players lose the first game he has coached? Certainly not, if he wants to make a career out of coaching! A good coach knows that practice and perseverance are vital. We have to practice our newly acquired tools regularly. Again,

I defer to Vince's coaching wisdom: "Once you learn to quit, it becomes a habit."

If a football team is losing at half-time, does the coach stay for the second half? A good coach not only stays, but brainstorms and analyzes new ideas for the second half. We have to recognize that every day is not going to be perfect. Instead of walking away, we do our best.

While there are many other successful skills of coaching, these offer a good primer. I have summarized them below.

Think about the past seven days. How did you treat yourself? Did you use more positive or negative coaching responses?

Positive Self-Coaching Response	Negative Self-Coaching Response
Expect that the best will happen.	Have no expectations or low expectations.
Use our "attitude tools" day-in and day-out, regardless of convenience or mood.	Use our "attitude tools" only when convenient or we "feel like it."
Assess our progress and performance in a constructive way.	Belittle our accomplishments and focus on our shortcomings.
When we stumble, get back on track with our attitude toolbox as soon as possible.	When we stumble, just quit.
Understand everything is a process.	Expect change overnight.

Logically, the concept of coaching ourselves in a positive way makes perfect sense. Yet we still keep repeating self-defeating behaviors. Why?

ɡood news: You are a wonderful learner. Despite anything you believe or have been told, you learn quickly and practice what you learn consistently.

The bad news: You have learned some of the "wrong ways" to think.

While our schools teach reading, writing, and arithmetic, we are left on our own to learn how to think. Unfortunately, there are many people in this world who believe the quickest way to build themselves up is by pushing someone else down. Most of our childhood years (and sometimes into college, marriage, and our occupations) we are associating with these people. During our fundamental years when we had to learn how to think, they were our examples. We learned from them — and we learned well.

Here is another question: if you knew English, could you also learn Spanish?

The answer is an obvious yes. Just because you know one language, does not mean you cannot learn another. Actually, the fact that you know English demonstrates your ability to learn a language! Likewise, you can learn a different way of thinking. But just like learning a new language, it won't happen overnight but with consistent effort, it *will* happen.

In any moment you have the power to choose what you think about.
You can't think about two things at once.
When you think about something negative,
you will produce negative feelings or actions.
When you think about something positive,
you will produce positive feelings or actions.

TAKE A STEP FORWARD

Copy the paragraph above on a Personal Power Card. On the back of the card, write down how you can use this knowledge to help you. When discouraging thoughts enter your mind, replace the thought. Use Self-Coaching techniques to seek out the positive.

worn-out woman step 4

FIGHTING BACK FATIGUE
A One-Step Plan to Begin
Reclaiming Lost Energy

"It is always too early to quit."—*Norman Vincent Peale*

I have noticed over the past decade a growing tendency "to be tired." In the past week how many people (yourself included) have you heard say: "I am tired," or "I didn't make much progress today," or "I just couldn't sleep last night," or "I'll have to get to this next week. I was sick/tired (or sick and tired)." On the flipside, how many people have exclaimed: "I woke up feeling great!" or "Wow! I had a productive day."

When we hear people speak these tired phrases, the most common response is: "Really? I didn't sleep well either..." or some other empathetic statement that confirms our own fatigue. We may even find ourselves one-upping another person: "You think you're tired..."

Walking around occasionally/constantly tired has become the norm, and we look at those with high-energy as the exception. In a recent survey, one out of two adults reported that fatigue interferes with their quality of life. For some, these interferences are big: missed work, depression, health problems. For others these symptoms manifest in smaller ways. Either way, these adults unanimously felt that reducing fatigue would dramatically improve quality of life.

Quality sleep radically affects daily functioning, and physical and mental health.

Lack of quality sleep:

- Causes irritability and unhappiness
- Causes thinking processes to slow down
- Decreases focus and attention
- Increases prevalence of depression (some experts think depression after childbirth, postpartum blues, is caused, in part, by a lack of sleep)
- Increases confusion
- Increases stress
- Impairs immune system which weakens the ability to fight off common infections
- Negatively affects the vascular system
- Increases appetite and risk for obesity (people who report an average total sleep time of five hours a night, for example, are much more likely to become obese compared to people who sleep seven to eight hours a night)
- Negatively affects blood sugar levels (when healthy young men slept only four hours a night for six nights in a row, their insulin and blood sugar levels mimicked those seen in people who were developing diabetes)
- Increases odds of strokes, irregular heartbeat, heart attacks, and congestive heart failure
- Leads to faulty decision-making and more risk-taking
- Reduces reaction time
- Increases likelihood of developing diabetes

> *When people who lack sleep are tested by using a driving simulator, they perform just as poorly as people who are drunk.*

SLEEPING TOWARD SUCCESS

For many, energy is like happiness. You keep chasing it and just when you think you have it cornered, it sneaks out a window and the search begins again. But there's a simple way to start hanging on to it—sleep. The National Institutes of Health is right on the mark when it says, "Sleep is as essential for your well-being as food and water."

Sleep is very similar to food, in that we can make healthy choices or poor choices. Our physical (and mental) results will rest on these choices. Yet, the science of sleep has recently evolved in dramatic ways and many of us don't know what a healthy choice is. Sure, there is the commonly stated guideline of "Get eight hours of sleep," but when? And what if we don't need that many? What if we need more? Can we sleep ten hours one night—will that change anything?

ABANDONING ROUTINES

When healthy adults are allowed to sleep unrestricted, the average time slept is eight to eight-and-a-half hours. Some people need more than that to avoid problem sleepiness; others need less. If a person does not get enough sleep, even on one night, a "sleep debt" begins to build.

Many people believe they can make up for lost sleep the following night—or following week. These people tend to "crash," whether by performing poorly in their day-to-day functions or "hitting the wall" and feeling utterly exhausted, needing several days or longer to "recoup." (I was once part of this latter group and would push the limits of my energy, only to need three to four days of complete "me time" after four to five weeks.) Few people would choose to skip eating one day and eat double the next, or skip eating for a week and "make up for it next week." Sleep is similar to food in this way; sleep deficits cannot be "filled later." Until sleep is regulated, optimal energy is not possible.

Changing sleep patterns on weekends or vacations throws off the body's internal clock, just like travel. If you live on the West Coast and normally have breakfast at 8:00 a.m., but sleep in three hours later on the weekend and have breakfast at 11:00 a.m., you might as well have traveled to New York. No wonder it is harder to dislodge yourself from the bed come Monday. You are creating "mini jet lags" again and again.

TOO MUCH TO DO?

When people are asked why they aren't getting enough sleep, the average person will answer, "I have too much to do." Skipping sleep actually reduces our ability to get things done. A 2003 report showed that a 10 percent increase in overtime worked created a 2.5 percent decrease in productivity. When people work over sixty hours a week, performance can decrease as much as 25 percent. A Cornell University study discovered that reduced productivity and fatigue-related accidents cost U.S. industry $150 billion dollars per year. Whether primary work is in an office, factory, on the road, or at home, this decrease in performance creates the need for additional time to correct or to complete the work. Additional time means less sleep. And so the cycle begins, often with caffeine helping people "ride the rollercoaster."

TAKE A STEP FORWARD

Set a time to wake in the morning and go to sleep in the evening. Each day, including weekends, go to bed at the *same* time. Each morning, including weekends, *wake* at the same time. Adhere to your designated wake and sleep time daily. When special circumstances interrupt your typical pattern, instead of skipping the sleep, try to add the lost sleep within the next twenty-four hours by taking a nap during the day or going to bed earlier. If that is not possible, know your energy, focus, and attitude may be affected. Resuming your regular schedule as soon as possible will put you back on track within just a couple of days.

Note: Science has revealed our biological clock is optimized to gain the most benefit from sleep between 10:00 p.m. and 4:00 a.m.. If possible, sleep during those hours. If you are a nightshift worker, please visit http://www.brooknoelstudio.com for science and tips to help you recover energy.

worn-out woman step 5

Creating Personal Power Scripts

"As long as one keeps searching, the answers come." —*Joan Baez*

Personal power scripts and affirmative statements (or affirmations) are positively phrased sentences in the present tense. We strip out the "I should, I will, I'm going to..." and replace with empowering words like "I am." Perhaps you have tried using affirmative statements in the past and haven't seen any dramatic differences from their use. I am going to encourage you to try them again. Using affirmative statements alone rarely produces lasting or sustaining change. It is the combination of affirmative statements with the other techniques you are learning that creates transformation.

I am going to use the example of health to demonstrate how affirmative statements, when designed correctly, change the mind's perspective.

Example A: A woman is full of unhealthy habits that she wants to change. Month after month she says, "I want to become healthier." When her favorite dessert is passed around at a dinner party, she takes some. Why? Because she *wants* to become healthier—at some point! **Not today.** She sees that in *her future,* not in *her now.* As long as that remains in her future, there is not any compelling reason to give up the short-term gratification in the present.

Example B: The same unhealthy woman says, "I am a healthy person." (An affirmative statement.) At that same dinner party, when her favorite dessert is passed, she doesn't take any. Why? Because *she is* a healthy person. She has already pictured herself as healthy, and become healthy by affirming it. She's not taking action tomorrow; she's taking action right now.

The differences between the woman in Example A and Example B are very subtle. Woman B did not need to go out and buy a membership to a club, or revamp her cupboards, or purchase expensive exercise equipment or diet plans. *She changed her thinking, and her thinking changed her action.*

I want to share with you where I believe affirmations derive their power from.

Imagine this scene with me:

You have been working late every night for two weeks. Your six-year-old child desperately wants to go to the park with you and play on the new swing set that was installed over the weekend.

When she asks, "Can we pleeeeeeaase go to the park tonight?" with her big blue eyes, you respond:

"I am not sure, honey. I may have a dinner tonight, but I will try my best."

Compare that response with this one:

"Sure honey. Tonight I will take you to the park."

Now let's fast-forward in your day. You are just about to leave the office when someone comes in who really needs your help. You know the person could complete this task without you, but your help would greatly simplify the process. The decision you make in this moment will likely be influenced by your response to your daughter earlier this morning.

If you said, "I will try. I may have a dinner tonight, but I will do my best." You will likely feel a strong push-and-pull between leaving and staying. You did not make a true commitment or affirmative statement to your child.

However if you said, "Yes. Tonight I am taking you to the park," you would be more likely to explain to the coworker you have a prior commitment.

Why? Because the second statement, "Yes. Tonight I am taking you to the park," is an affirmative statement. In essence, *you gave someone your word.*

Do you know what starts the majority of disagreements and miscommunications between people? *People get upset when a person says one thing, but does another.* We don't like to have to go back on our word, and we don't it like when other people do so either. When we use an affirmative statement, we put our word on the line. Our mind will do everything it can to position ourselves for the realization of that statement.

Studies have shown that those who use written affirmations are 86 percent more likely to accomplish what they have written than those who do not use written affirmative statements. I don't know about you, but with odds like that, I think I can find the time to speak affirmatively and write it down!

HOW TO USE AFFIRMATIVE PERSONAL POWER SCRIPTS

In my self-work and work with other women, I have found that writing down negative thoughts as they surface and replacing them with positive affirmative statements is a powerful step. I encourage you to keep your index cards near you throughout the day. Whenever you have a negative thought or doubt, write it down in sentence form on one side of the card. On the backside of the card, write a positive affirmative statement. Spend time reviewing your deck, looking only at the one side containing the positive statements.

Here are some common negative statements I have collected in my work along with examples of affirmative statements to contradict them.

Negative Statement	Positive Statement
I am not good enough.	I am enough.
I don't deserve ____ (fill in the blank).	I deserve happiness. Every moment I am stepping closer to where I want to be.
I'll never _____ (fill in the blank). or I can't _____.	I accomplish everything I set my mind to.
I'll deal with that in the future. I don't have the energy now.	My time is now. I find energy in challenges and deal with them effectively.
I will try to_____(fill in the blank).	I will_____(fill in the blank)
I am unlucky.	I determine my own destiny.
I'm a bad person.	I am a great person.
There is always tomorrow.	I am moving forward today.
Life has dealt me a bad hand.	I am in control of my own happiness
I'm a bad_____.(mother, friend, wife, employee, etc.)	I am doing my best every single day.
Oh well, such is life.	My life and happiness are up to me.

Here are three more affirmative statements that I personally love and keep with me daily:

I make today matter.

I can and I do.

I am enough.

TAKE A STEP FORWARD

Add Personal Power Cards to your deck by replacing negative scripts with affirmative, positive, power scripts. Carry one or two cards in the CAN self-adhesive pockets.

mini-makeover

Here's to Your Health!

"Health is a state of complete physical, mental and social well-being, and not merely the absence of disease or infirmity." —*World Health Organization, 1948*

Have you tried more than one diet or exercise regimen? More than ten? Have you been focusing on what you eat (counting grams, calories and points) instead of behavioral changes that last a life-time? This Mini-Makeover explores food, fitness and ideas you can implement to easily begin living a healthier life today.

Step 1: The Simplest Diet in the World

Step 2: That Meal in the Morning

Step 3: S.O.S. for Stress

Step 4: Let's Get Moving!

Step 5: Wading into Water

here's to your health!
step 1

The Simplest Diet in the World

"In two decades I've lost a total of 789 pounds. I should be hanging from a charm bracelet." —*Erma Bombeck*

You are about to learn three of the quickest, easiest, simplest ways to dramatically control your food consumption, and that of your entire family, without ever creating a "food plan" or banning a food. Ready?

RULE #1: ONLY EAT AT YOUR DINING ROOM TABLE AND DO NOT ENGAGE IN ACTIVITY EXCEPT THOUGHT OR CONVERSATION WHILE EATING.

This simple step can change your relationship with food. Often eating becomes an activity we do on auto-pilot. We snack at our computer. We eat in front of a television. We eat in the car. We sneak a bite here and there while preparing a meal. Eat whatever you like as long as you are sitting at the dining room table and not multitasking. You must remain focused on your food, thoughts, or conversation. No browsing a magazine, the paper, or the mail. No puzzle or Sudoku-solving, writing a grocery list, paging through a planner, or jotting down notes.

HOW THIS SIMPLE STEP CREATES RADICAL CHANGE

1. **We get in touch with our bodies.**

   When we avoid distracting our mind through multitasking, we can hear our body's cues. When we cease our mindless activity, we can hear the fullness cue. By implementing this behavioral change, food becomes either a source to feed the body, or a time we share with others in conversation. Food is not used as a backdrop for emotions or boredom.

2. **We are an impatient society.**

   The reason a person can eat "whatever they want" as long as she remains at the table is because we are an impatient society and easily bored. We do not want to sit at a table without stimuli; otherwise we would already be doing it. Many people have a hard time stopping and pausing. If we add up the amount of time we spend eating away from a table (including all grazing) it is often equal to or more than the time spent at the table. With this simple tool, most of us will find we would rather *feed our body* and leave the table than sit and consume more and more food.

RULE #2: NEVER EAT OUT OF A BAG OR BOX.

It is very easy to eat out of a bag or box and "accidentally" exceed the serving size listed on the package. We wonder why our weight loss attempts are ineffective: "I only had a few pretzels for lunch!" A few is not a metric measure. Each time you eat, take out the defined portion (see the packaging for serving size) and then place the remaining food back in the cabinet, pantry, or refrigerator. Go sit down and enjoy with the guidelines in Rule #1. If you finish and would like more, go ahead. Repeat the process, removing a single portion and putting the remaining food back.

RULE # 3: CHEW.

This rule has been around for a long time and is worth adding to the above two. Chew your food—completely. Finish one bite before taking another.

By following these three simple rules, without making any other changes, the majority of people will lose weight and drastically improve eating habits.

COMMON QUESTIONS

WHAT ABOUT DRIVE-THROUGH?

Sorry. No eating in the car. Either go in and sit down or save the food until you get home. The other option…pull into a parking lot or rest stop, turn off your car (you can leave the radio on if you like), and do not start the engine until you are done eating.

WHAT ABOUT WHEN I AM AT WORK AND THERE ISN'T A TABLE OR AREA TO EAT?

If you go out for lunch, eat at the restaurant. If you do not go out, and there is not a designated break area, turn off your phone and computer. If possible, close the door. Eat at your desk without looking at work or any other distractions.

WHAT ABOUT BEVERAGES?

Beverages are not included in the above (unless they are milkshakes!)

PARTICIPATION

While you can do this on your own, it is a great step toward healthy eating as a family. Encourage your family to join you!

TAKE A STEP FORWARD

Begin eating every meal and snack at the table with these guidelines. Encourage your family to adopt this as a new family rule. Watch the drastic changes that follow when mindless eating is eliminated.

TOOLS, RESOURCES, AND REFERENCES
- ☒ Visit the Rush Hour Meal Planning area for healthy (and quick) meal ideas.

here's to your health!
step 2

That Meal in the Morning

"All happiness depends on a leisurely breakfast." —*John Gunther*

In a now-famous study conducted by Ernesto Pollitt of the University of Texas Health Science Center, the performance of students who ate breakfast and those who did not were compared. His study revealed that those who ate breakfast made measurably fewer errors as the morning wore on. Additional studies performed on adults revealed the same results. Breakfast is vital to energy and focus.

Ideally, breakfast should contain complex carbohydrates and protein; for example, skim milk and a healthy cereal. At a minimum, you should grab something—a banana, a piece of plain whole-wheat toast or one with jam or jelly, a cereal bar not loaded with sugar.

What if I don't eat breakfast? You simply have to eat breakfast if you are going to maximize energy, metabolism, live a healthy lifestyle, and create a solid base. For years I didn't eat breakfast (unless you count coffee). I don't really enjoy eating breakfast even today, but I now understand the benefits of a healthy breakfast to energy, metabolism, and focus. These benefits outweigh my personal breakfast-avoidance tendency. I aim to consume breakfast within sixty minutes of waking to maximize benefits to the metabolism.

In addition to this kind of energy benefit, the Rutland Regional Medical Center in Vermont found:

- Eating breakfast is linked to a lower body mass, compared to people who skip the meal.
- Eating breakfast is shown to reduce a person's risk of obesity and insulin resistance.
- Eating breakfast is one of the few proven strategies to maintaining long-term weight loss.

In addition, the Nemours Foundation found people who eat breakfast tend to eat healthier throughout the day and often weigh less than people who skip the day's first meal. What you eat is important, so you should make healthy choices for breakfast. Try to eat lots of fruits, whole grains, and lean proteins. Eggs, fruit smoothies, and whole-grain pancakes, waffles, oatmeal, and cereals are healthy choices for breakfast.

If you're in a hurry, the Nemours Foundation suggests quick snacks like yogurt, fruit, or whole-grain muffins. For a healthy snack, try mixing cereal, pretzels, nuts, and dried fruit as opposed to prepackaged breakfast pastries or doughnuts that are high in fat and sugar.

SIMPLE, CONVENIENT, AND HEALTHY BREAKFAST CHOICES

HOT AND COLD CEREAL: CREATING YOUR OWN "CEREAL BAR"

There just isn't any way around it—cereal remains one of the number-one breakfast foods. And it makes sense: cereal lasts for a while in the cupboard, is quick and easy, and provides the well-balanced start we need for the day (as long as you pick the right cereal!). While a homemade smoothie, egg white omelet, or freshly-sliced fruit salad might provide more nutritional punch, we also have to consider convenience. For those people who are not morning people or those who don't eat breakfast because they "don't have the time," cereal is the quickest cure.

Brand Name	Calories	Total Fat	Sat. Fat	Cholesterol	Sodium	Carbs	Dietary Fiber	Protein	Sugars
Cheerios	111	1.8 g	.4 g	0	273 mg	22.2 g	2.7 g	3.3g	1.2g
Other notable traits: Meets 10% of the DRV (daily recommended value) for Vitamin A and C and Calcium. Meets 45% of Iron DRV.									
Kelloggs Special K	117	.5 g	.1 g	0	224 mg	22 g	0.7 g	7.0 g	4 g
Other notable traits: Meets 15% of the Vitamin A DRV, 35% of the Vitamin C DRV, 47% of Iron DRV									
TOTAL	100	.5	0	0	190 mg	23 g	3.0 g	2.0 g	5.0 g
Other notable traits Meets 100% of DRV in calcium, fiber, iron, niacin, riboflavin, Vitamins B6 and B12 (important for energy), Vitamin C and Zinc									
Kashi Heart to Heart	116	1.6 g	0	0	89 mg	24.9 g	4.9 g	4.4 g	4.9 g
Other notable traits: One of the healthiest cereals you'll find! And this is based not on 1 cup but 1 ¾ cups! Contains 25% of the DRV for Vitamin A and 49% of the DRV for Vitamin C.									

Let's take a look at some good cereal choices — each of these is based on one cup of dry cereal. In order for a cereal to be included as a "good choice," the maximum sugar allowed per cup was 5.0 grams, and that was only on TOTAL because it provides so many other benefits. This is just a glimpse at the labels on a few "good cereals" so you can see how they compare.

Many other cereals fall into this "good choice" group. Without listing the exact details of each cereal, here are others that meet our goals without a lot of sugar or artificial extras:

1. **Wheaties**

2. **Kix**

3. **All-Bran with Extra Fiber**

4. **Rice Krispies**

5. **Fiber One**

6. **Kellogg's Corn Flakes**

7. **Crispix**

8. **Most hot instant oatmeals**

9. **Cream of Wheat**

HOW DO I DETERMINE IF MY CEREAL WORKS?
Cereal Guidelines: for maximum energy without the high-and-low of a sugar rush, choose cereals with less than five grams of sugar per cup.

COMPLETING YOUR CEREAL BAR
Select a few different cereals that you like. In the morning have one cup of cereal with nonfat or skim milk (or 2% if you must!).
Top your cereal with one of the following:

1 cup strawberries
1 cup raspberries
1 cup blackberries
1 cup blueberries
½ banana

If you do not like to top cereal with fruit, have it on the side or opt for one of the following:

1 apple
1 orange
½ grapefruit
1 cup of fresh melon
1 cup of grapes

All in all, the one cup of cereal will have around one hundred calories, the milk another one hundred calories, and the fruit around one hundred calories. Add a glass of water and you end up with a perfect three-hundred-calorie energy-optimized breakfast.

OTHER OPTIONS

SCRAMBLED EGGS AND WHOLE WHEAT TOAST

2 eggs, scrambled
1 slice of whole wheat toast (dry or use butter spray)

Feel free to prepare your eggs over easy or any other way you like! Just make sure to use a non-stick cooking spray instead of butter in the pan.

General health notes

While eggs are high in protein and a good source of fuel for many, they are also high in cholesterol and saturated fat. If you are following a low-cholesterol diet, consider one of the other choices. Generally, do not choose eggs more than two times per week. Consider using egg substitutes versus eggs to avoid the cholesterol, but keep in mind that egg substitutes are higher in sodium.

WAFFLES TOPPED WITH FRUIT
Fast, quick, and easy! (You can also purchase pancakes with similar nutrient values.)

3 Eggo Special K Waffles (190 calories)
1 cup strawberries, blueberries, or raspberries (49 calories)
½ cup fat-free yogurt (50 calories and a great source of protein)

Mix berries and yogurt while toasting waffles. Top waffles with yogurt and fruit mixture. Low on sugar, adds fiber, vitamins, and protein!

MORNING SMOOTHIE BREAKFAST

½ frozen banana (This is a great use for overripe bananas—peel bananas, cut in half, and freeze.)

½ cup frozen strawberries, blackberries, blueberries, raspberries, or combo
1 (8 ounce) container nonfat plain/vanilla yogurt
½ cup orange juice

Mix in a blender and serve immediately. You can add a handful of ice cubes if you like, although the frozen fruit serves as a way to make the smoothie cold and fresh, while still being creamy like a milkshake.

COTTAGE CHEESE, TOAST, AND FRUIT COMBO

1 cup low-fat (1%) cottage cheese
½ cup strawberries
2 pieces reduced calorie toasted wheat bread like Healthy Choice with butter spray

MORE GREAT BREAKFAST RECIPES

A nice selection of recipes, including breakfast recipes, can be accessed in this free recipe book: http://www.4women.gov/ body-works/toolkit/recipebook.pdf

TAKE A STEP FORWARD

Commit to eating breakfast within sixty minutes of waking. Choose a meal option that is appealing and convenient. Maintain this practice daily for maximum energy and health.

TOOLS, RESOURCES, AND REFERENCES
☑ View additional breakfast ideas online.
☒ Visit the Meal Planning area of the member site for weekly breakfast plans complete with recipes and shopping lists.

here's to your health! step 3

S.O.S. for Stress

"In health there is freedom. Health is the first of all liberties." —*Henri Frederic Amiel*

While stress is not as easy to measure as a heart rate, it is a leading cause of illness and a primary reason people have difficulty implementing or maintaining healthy lifestyle choices.

Stress is triggered by a lack of resources (time, skills, or people) to meet perceived demands. When we feel pressured to handle a situation immediately, most women will find time by neglecting self-care and healthy habits. A short-term solution, this becomes a catch-22 over time. By skipping self-care we reduce our physical and emotional resources, making it harder to cope with a stressful situation. So what's a gal to do?

While eliminating all stress would be ideal, it isn't a realistic solution in this day and age. When we cannot eliminate something, we need to learn to live with and manage it instead. Taking steps to proactively minimize stress while increasing our awareness and coping mechanisms can drastically reduce the impact of stress on our bodies and health.

Studies have linked stress to headaches, heart disease, intensifying existing asthma, gastrointestinal problems, and chronic pain.

UNDERSTANDING STRESS

First the good news: stress is not a result of the challenges you face in life, but of your perception of these challenges. Why is that good news? We cannot control life events but we can definitely influence and alter our perceptions. Perception explains why an event can be stressful to one person, but not another; for example, I love public speaking yet I know many people who are filled with stress at the thought of a pending speech. I become stressed out in tornado watches and warnings, yet I have a friend who loves to look outside during these bad weather times.

TOP FIVE STRESSORS

- Worrying about health
- Worrying about finances
- Lack of sleep
- Stressed from workload
- Too many outside commitments

A QUICK STRESS TEST

Below is a list of common symptoms of stress. Circle any of the following that are currently present in your life or have been in the past thirty days.

Simple Stress Test

Headaches	Racing thoughts	Insomnia
Fatigue	Defensiveness	Frequent illness
Grinding teeth	Clenched jaw	Chest pain
High blood pressure	Pounding heart	Indigestion

Anxiety	Sadness	Increased perspiration
Poor job performance		Overeating or loss of appetite

Total _____

To complete this informal stress test, count up how many circles you have and then find the category you fit into from the following options:

If you circled 5 or less = While you can benefit from learning stress-reduction and coping techniques, your stress level is in the ideal range.

If you circled between 6 and 11 = Stress is definitely detracting from your overall quality of life and could become a health threat if you do not proactively deal with your stressors.

If you circled 12 or more = You are in the high-stress category. Pay special attention to the coping suggestions of this lesson.

COPING WITH STRESS

UNDERSTAND YOUR STRESS TRIGGERS
Each of us is "set off" by unique events. Spend a week acting like a detective and noting when your stress level rises. Write down your findings in your journal or CAN.

BECOME PROACTIVE
For each area you identified as a stressor, brainstorm possible options and solutions. It is better to create a routine that avoids stress than to cope with it. For example, if you continually find yourself stressed in the morning trying to get everyone and every-thing ready and out the door, take thirty minutes at night to prepare

so you can avoid the panicked morning rush. If you have a hard time thinking of solutions, brainstorm ideas with a friend or family member.

DON'T TRY TO SOLVE EVERYTHING OVERNIGHT
Once you discover your triggers and proactive plans, do not try to implement them all right away. Trying to do so will likely cause more stress. Instead, start with your biggest stressor and make one change each week in that area. Make sure that change is helping and then add another.

THE OUTLOOK FACTOR

Whether you call it optimism or pessimism or attitude, outlook refers to the general "lens" through which we see the world. Each of us looks at every experience differently, based on our unique history. Those people who view the world in a pessimistic way tend to have more stress and greater health problems. Many studies have been done on how attitude affects overall health. While the specific impact varies, most all studies concur that those people who are more positive live longer and have less risk of heart disease—or if they do contract heart disease, have a better chance of recovering.

Like stress, our attitude is based on our perception of events. Again, this is good news. While we cannot always change the events of our life, we do have control over our perception. Retraining ourselves is not an overnight task, but diligent attention and focus over time can retrain your thinking.

AM I AN OPTIMIST OR A PESSIMIST?
Here is a quick self-assessment tool you can use to determine whether you are an optimist or a pessimist.

Think of the last time that you faced a challenge or problem. Choose which phrases best described your thought process during that time.

Did you...

A	**B**
Assume that it was a problem created by various people and circumstances.	Assume that it was all *your* fault.
Realize that "this too shall pass."	Feel that it would last forever.
Understand that while this area might be troublesome, it needn't affect other areas of your life.	Let the problem affect all areas of your life.

Now think of a time when you realized a success. Which phrase best describes your thought process during that successful period:

A	**B**
I realized I worked hard and made it happen.	I felt that "I got lucky."
I knew that this was just one of many successes I would realize in my life.	I didn't expect another success.

And now a few more questions about how you look at things day to day. Place a checkmark in either the A or B column.

WHAT YOUR SCORE MEANS

If you have more As than Bs you tend to mostly hold an optimistic viewpoint. If you have more Bs than As you tend to mostly hold a pessimistic viewpoint. If the number of A's and B's are close, then

Phrase	Agree A	Disagree B
When I face something unexpected during the day I can easily regroup and refocus without letting the day become derailed.		
When someone gives me feedback, I interpret it objectively and don't automatically assume they are criticizing me.		
I rarely feel sorry for myself and instead appreciate what I do have.		
I rarely complain and don't like to be around people who do complain.		
When I face a problem, instead of giving up or becoming depressed, I brainstorm solutions.		
I give thanks daily for all of life's little and big blessings.		
I believe that I can accomplish my goals and dreams.		
All in all there are twelve sections in the Outlook self-assessment. Please total the number of A's you have and the number of B's you have and record them on this line.		

you tend to be optimistic in certain areas and circumstances and pessimistic in other areas.

TAKE A STEP FORWARD

Begin by completing the stress test and using the proactive technique to journal ways you can alleviate stressors.

In the Outlook Factor section, for any question you answered with a B, journal about when and where you most often face these types of situations. For example: *When I face something unexpected during the day I can easily regroup and refocus without letting the day become derailed.* Do you most often experience that sense of derailment at work, at home, on a personal goal or project? Try to identify the areas that most commonly trouble you. Then try some of the techniques that follow for improving your outlook.

KEEP A GRATITUDE JOURNAL
Each day list five to ten things that you are grateful for, no matter how simple or small. Focusing on what is good in life tends to attract more good. Also, when we stay focused on the positives in life, we can better keep the challenges in perspective.

AUDIT THE SITUATION
Before going into a full-fledged negative reaction, take a quick time-out and ask: "What exactly is happening here?" and "How will stress, anxiety, anger, or negativity help me move forward? What are some other choices I could make?"

PUT PESSIMISM ON THE CLOCK
Instead of becoming derailed for a day, week, or more, put pessimism on the clock. Give yourself twenty minutes to really complain or have a pity-party about the matter at hand. Then spend thirty minutes brainstorming a solution. We tend to feel the worst when we choose to not to think about options available to us. Brainstorming options helps relieve negativity.

USE AFFIRMATIVE STATEMENTS
Create some affirmation cards with positive statements about yourself in the present tense. Example: *Each day I am getting better and better!* Purposely feed your mind positive statements to help counteract the negative. Positive-thinking expert Norman Vincent Peale determined it takes twenty-seven positive statements to counteract one negative statement.

LIMIT NEGATIVE EXPOSURE
Being around other negative people or situations can kick-start or increase your negativity. Refuse to engage with others who are

negative or who gossip. Minimize exposure to negative music, television, and reading. Replace sad music with positive audiobooks, replace negative reading with positive reading materials and motivational books.

TOOLS, RESOURCES, AND REFERENCES
☑ Additional copies of the worksheets in this Step can be printed online.

here's to your health!
step 4

Let's Get Moving!

"Health is the vital principle of bliss, and exercise, of health." —*James Thomson*

Welcome to a very short Step in our journey—a Step on exercise. I am not going to make this more complicated than it needs to be. The more we move, the healthier our mind and body become and the more energy we have. Exercise and movement release stress, increase metabolism, improve circulation, strengthen bones, tone muscles, and reduce health risks.

However, you may be surprised to know that you don't need to run to the gym for an hour each day to experience the energy-enhancing benefits of movement and exercise. A recent *Prevention* article shared how doing just ten minutes of LIGHT weight lifting repetitions caused a focus group to feel a 45 percent increase in their energy level. Pick up some light weights (five to ten pounds) at your local discount-mart, and start your day with ten minutes of your energetic playlist and moving the weights around. Don't have any weights? Grab some heavy cans, or fill some half-gallon containers. Just try it. When you get up in the morning don't think about exercise—instead exercise while you think. All of us have ten minutes a day. If you do not currently exercise regularly, begin by exercising three days a week. The goal is not to see how many days we can exercise consecutively, but how often we can exercise within our regular schedule. Aim for three days a week for ten minutes.

When you create a consistent framework you achieve the most challenging task of any exercise regimen—committing your time and resources regularly to move exercise from "good idea" to reality.

IDEAS FOR MOVEMENT

- Turn on some music and dance.
- Put on headphones with energetic music and head out the door walking. After five minutes, turn around and walk back to your home. If you need coffee during these ten minutes, take it with you.
- Take ten minutes to stretch or walk in place.

TAKE A STEP FORWARD

Brainstorm how, when, and what you are going to do to make time for your ten minutes of exercise three times each week. Record the day you will begin on your calendar. Write a paragraph to yourself about why you will commit to doing this for at least a few weeks. Then write down excuses you think you might use to try and get out of it. "Talk back" to your excuses by writing down sentences and solutions to overcome them.

TOOLS, RESOURCES, AND REFERENCES

- ☒ Join in an online sprint in our online member Action Jam Room. Supportive participants are ready to help you get started and stay accountable!
- ☑ If you are looking for a complete Health Makeover consider my *Health Challenge* program for a step-by-step fitness and nutrition makeover. Follow the website link to learn more.

here's to your health
step 5

Wading into Water

"Water is the lifeblood of our bodies, our economy, our nation and our well-being." —*Stephen Johnson*

Trivia question: How much water do experts recommend we consume daily? If you replied with "Eight, eight-ounce glasses per day," you are correct. Second question: What is the origin of this sixty-four-ounce guideline? Most people answer with "Well, everybody just knows that," or "the government."

At my last doctor visit I asked where this sixty-four-ounce water guideline originated. My doctor was stumped! I decided to do my own research since the sixty-four-ounce rule seems to be interpreted in so many ways: some sources include caffeinated beverages, others only count noncaloric beverages. Shortly after my doctor visit I discovered CNN had the same question. The news channel scouted for the source of the guideline:

"This eight, eight-ounce glasses a day, it turns out, after talking to the USDA, the National Academy of Sciences, the National Institutes of Health, people at various universities, they say, you know what, this appears to be kind of a myth. We can't find a single study that says that that's what people ought to do."

While experts may debate how much water we really need and what counts as water, everyone agrees that water is essential to

THREE CONSIDERATIONS FOR INTERPRETING HEALTH "FACTS"

These are only guidelines: Numbers, even well-researched and studied government numbers, are, in most cases, general guidelines for an average person. This means people's needs were spread over a wide range of numbers and this is the "middle number." Maybe you are the "average person," but maybe you are not. For example, I know that if I ate all the fat allotted to me on the Recommended Dietary Allowance I would be way above my recommended weight.

Numbers are relative: Most guidelines and facts are related to a group with specific characteristics. The physical makeup of this group is rarely released in mass media along with the guideline itself. Recently on a very well-known news channel, I learned ice cream was not only healthy, but could actually help a person lose weight! Assuming I must be dreaming, I went to check it out, as I do any alleged statistic before accepting it as fact. Twenty minutes later I was writing the network a "Shame on You Letter." The study was based on twenty-four men, studied over a period of eight weeks. I can't remember the average age or weight, but I guarantee you it did not match the majority of the viewership. The moral of the story: Identify what physical makeup numbers are based on before implementing personal changes based on the findings.

Just like interest, statistics can compound over time: How much water to drink, how much coffee is safe, how much fish to eat—as we adapt a guideline and pass it on and on and on and on again, we often lose the relative information. The statistic somehow becomes fact and like my doctor, we cannot identify the source. When the source is lost it is important to revisit current information. Science and research are always evolving and new information might mean it is time for a new "fact."

health and energy. Self-experimentation can help you discover the amount of water that is best for you.

HOW MUCH WATER?

How much water you actually need depends upon many variables. Among the key determinates are:

- Medications you are taking
- Geographic region
- Sweating
- Exercise and physical activity level
- Personal tendency toward dehydration
- The foods you eat

THE BASICS

Every system in your body is dependent on water. Ignoring water is like ignoring the oil change on your car. It will keep running — but for how long and how well?

With water we can use some average numbers to account for "output." Most adults excrete about two and a half liters of water a day. In order to avoid dehydration, we have to "put back" what we use. Assuming we are average, it would take eight cups of water to replace these two and a half liters. There are eight liquid ounces in one cup. Voila — eight x eight = sixty-four, the magic number.

VARIABLE: FOOD

A well-balanced diet replenishes about 20 percent of our water use. However, if you aren't eating a well-balanced diet (as defined by the Food Pyramid, www.mypryamid.gov), then you need to add a bit of water on top of your usual water intake. As a starting point, add twelve ounces of water if you do not eat a diet rich in fruits and vegetables.

IS YOUR WATER SAFE?

The last component of the water mystery is to make sure that the water you are drinking is *safe*. Here are government guidelines and resources to help you investigate your water options:

Think about the water you drink. Whether it's from your tap or from a bottle, find out where the water you drink comes from and whether it has been made safe to drink.

If you are getting your water from a public water system, find out if a Consumer Confidence Report (CCR) exists for your water system. http:// www.cdc.gov/ncidod/dpd/healthywater/public.htm

If you are an owner or user of a private well, make sure that your well is properly constructed, maintained, and tested. Visit our Private Well Resource Page for more information.

If you have questions about bottled water, make sure you are informed about where your bottled water comes from and how it has been treated. The standards for bottled water are set by the Food and Drug Administration (FDA). The FDA bases its standards on the Environmental Protection Agency (EPA) standards for tap water.

- Visit the FDA site for information on the different types of waters. In addition, read the label on your bottled water. This label can tell you about the way the bottled water is treated.
- Check the label for an 800 number or Web page address of the company that bottled the water. This may be a place to get further information.
- Visit the website of the International Bottled Water Association (IBWA), which represents many of the U.S. water bottlers.

VARIABLE: EXERCISE

If you exercise for under an hour at low to moderate intensity, eight to sixteen ounces of water will replace what is lost through sweating during exercise. If you think you sweat more than the average person, go for the higher range. The more intense the activity, the more replacement ounces needed. If you are walking at a leisurely pace, eight ounces might be sufficient, whereas a "power walk" may require sixteen. For exercise, I have found that using sweat as your guide is the best measure. For example, when the weather is warm, we need more water. Also, one person might work up a sweat at a slow walking pace, while another may not.

VARIABLE: ENVIRONMENT

When it is hot or humid we need extra fluid if we are outside. Additionally those living in altitudes of more than 8200 feet who notice increased urination need to up their liquid intake.

VARIABLE: HEALTH

Common conditions such as fever, flu, and diarrhea result in rapid fluid loss. It is important to increase fluid intake during such times. Yet other conditions such as adrenal diseases can cause the need to actually reduce fluid intake. If you have a health condition, make sure to check with your doctor for any fluid-specific guidelines. Lastly, if you are breastfeeding, the Institute of Medicine recommends increasing your fluid by thirty-two ounces.

TAKE A STEP FORWARD

To determine your water quota, begin with the golden-number "replacement theory" of sixty-four ounces, unless you regularly eat a diet high in fruits and veggies—then you can deduct 20 percent and start at fifty-two ounces.

	64 oz.	52 oz.
Starting Number		
Breastfeeding? Add 32 ounces	_____	_____
Any health conditions? + / − based on doctor recommendation	_____	_____
Live in warm climate and outdoors often? add 8–16 ounces	_____	_____
Live at an altitude over 8200 ft.? add 8–16 ounces	_____	_____
Total	_____	_____

This is your baseline number. Add an additional eight to sixteen ounces for each hour of exercise. Each day aim to consume your calculated water amount. If you currently drink very little water, begin slowly and add six ounces daily for one week, then another six, and continue until you reach your calculated number.

mini-makeover

Housework Helpers

"I hate housework. You make the beds, you wash the dishes and six months later you have to start all over again."—*Joan Rivers*

In this Mini-Makeover you will learn how to formulate a game plan to manage household maintenance: we'll create a Master Task List, learn a Simple Six-Box Sort and Stow Solution, recreate the dinner hour with Rush-Hour™ meal plans, and implement a daily sprint system to keep it all under control.

Step 1: Master Maintenance Schedule

Step 2: Sprint Your Way to Success

Step 3: Merge and Purge: The Six-Box System

Step 4: Create Your Master Task List

Step 5: Mastering Meal Planning

Specific Supplies:
- Four large RubberMaid (or other brand of your choice) plastic tubs. (You can save money by using cardboard boxes, although I find a durable tub to be a better choice.) Choose a large tub, ten- to twenty-gallon. Make sure it has comfortable handles. Choose a tub that if filled, you could still carry comfortably.

- A three-ring binder to hold recipes and page protectors to keep safe from spills.

housework helpers
step 1

Master Maintenance Schedule

"Nothing is particularly hard if you divide it into small jobs."—*Henry Ford*

When our homes are in disarray, our attitude suffers. It is hard to get the day started on the right foot when you cannot locate the shoe for that foot. You know how it feels to walk into a home with papers piled everywhere, and dust bunnies on the loose—stress levels begin to rise. Take the same home, purge, clean, and control, and what was once a source of stress becomes a source of peace and pride.

The first step in taking control involves doing as Ford advises and dividing a large task into smaller components. In the *Change Your Life Challenge,* we use the Housework Helpers Worksheet as the foundation for Weekly and Monthly Master Task Lists.

HOW TO COMPLETE THE HOUSEWORK HELPERS WORKSHEET

Begin in the room of your choice. During this process you will walk through your entire home, so you may want to begin at one end and work toward the other. (This needs to be a physical walk-through—not completed in your head.)

Housework Helpers Worksheet

DESCRIPTION	TASKS DONE ONCE A WEEK OR MORE							TASKS DONE LESS THAN WEEKLY BUT AT LEAST MONTHLY			TASKS DONE LESS THAN ONCE A MONTH					
	1	2	3	4	5	6	7	1X	2X	3x	BIMONTHLY	QUARTERLY	BIANNUALLY	YEARLY	MERGE AND PURGE

UNDERSTANDING THE HOUSEWORK HELPERS WORKSHEET

The far-left column is used for recording a task. The next columns are numbered one through seven to represent the seven days of a week. If a task is done once a week, a checkmark would be placed in the "one" column. If a task is done three times per week, a checkmark would be placed in the "three" column. A task performed once a day would receive a mark in the "seven" column.

In the next column, choices include every other week, monthly, every other month, quarterly, twice per year, and annually. Any task not performed weekly would receive a checkmark in one of these columns.

In the end, each task should have one checkmark in the column whose frequency most matches the task. Aim for satisfaction, not perfection. As you examine each task ask: how often does this really need to be done, in order for me to feel satisfied with the result?

THE MERGE AND PURGE COLUMN

The last column on the Housework Helpers is the merge and purge column. A merge and purge is similar to spring cleaning. Sometimes an area gets cluttered, overloaded, or otherwise disorganized. To restore it to a maintenance-friendly area, a merge and purge is required. For example, if you are standing in front of your bookshelves and determine regular dusting is needed, yet cannot see the shelves due to miscellaneous piles, a merge and purge is required. Other areas in your home may not need regular cleaning, but only a merge and purge. For example, few people make a regular practice of emptying and wiping down every drawer in the home routinely. However if we have a drawer that no longer closes, or a junk drawer filled with clutter, at some point we will want to perform a merge and purge. A task can have a checkmark in only the merge-and-purge column, or a checkmark in the merge-and purge-column and a routine maintenance frequency column.

THE KEY TO SUCCESS

Breaking jobs down into manageable components is the key to any effective system. Listing "clean kitchen" as a task is not effective. Cleaning the kitchen is likely comprised of many different tasks, some done daily, others three times per week, some quarterly, and others yearly.

Instead of "clean kitchen," specific tasks would be listed; for example:

- Sweep kitchen floor
- Mop kitchen floor
- Empty and load dishwasher
- Wipe down counters
- Clean inside of microwave
- Clean out refrigerator
- Clean freezer
- Wipe down and clean small appliances
- Clean oven
- Wipe down cabinets

Consider using a separate worksheet for each major room in your home. For like rooms, such as multiple bathrooms, you may want to list tasks done in all bathrooms at the top of a worksheet, then list out bathroom one, bathroom two, bathroom three, and room-specific tasks.

TAKE A STEP FORWARD

Walk through your home and list cleaning tasks on the Housework Helpers Worksheet. Do not forget hallways, staircase landings, laundry rooms, or overstuffed closets. In the Step to come, we will cover how to work through both cleaning and merge-and-purge tasks.

TOOLS, RESOURCES, AND REFERENCES
   ☑ Additional copies of the Housework Helpers Worksheet are available on the website.

housework helpers
step 2

Sprint Your Way to Success

"A rock pile ceases to be a rock pile the moment a single man contemplates it, bearing within him the image of a cathedral." —*Antoine de Saint-Exupery*

Thousands of women who have joined our online community for sprinting sessions have been amazed at how much can be done with a timer and a ten- to twenty-minute block of focused energy.

Using a timer to "make a dent" is the quickest way to get past a feeling of dread and turn the insurmountable into the conquerable. If you have a *Change Your Life Challenge* timer, you are all set. If you do not, you can order one online or pick up a timer at a kitchen store, pharmacy, or discount store.

Why not an oven timer, like we've used earlier in this book? It is important the timer is easily portable, otherwise you may not hear the timer ding at the end of the sprint. Look for a simple-to-use timer that can also be clipped onto your waist comfortably.

I began a ten-minute sprint in the morning a number of years ago, quite by accident. The auto-timer on my coffeemaker quit working. Each morning, instead of waking to fresh brew, I came downstairs and had to hit the brew button. This particular coffeemaker took its sweet time to generate my java—about ten minutes. At first, I would watch the coffee brew. After a month I no longer found this entertaining. I decided to challenge myself and see how many things I could accomplish while my coffee brewed.

WANTED: HOUSEKEEPING APPRECIATION

One of the reasons many women loathe housework is because it is never ending. Undoubtedly, as soon as the dining room table is cleared and the laundry hamper is empty, we turn to find a new pile on the table or in the hamper. Like any repetitive task, efforts are rarely noticed by those we live with. It would be rare for a woman to hear, "Wow Mom! What a great sweeping job!" This never ending and underappreciated task isn't very attractive.

In our online program we began Housework Helpers Sprints. The experiment involved bringing women together online in a safe chat environment. The leader, who was me at the time, would have a timer, and each woman would identify an area they planned to focus on. I would do the grand countdown and twenty minutes later we all met back at our computer screens to report on our progress. It did not take long to see three things happened during these times:

1. Women recognized and praised each other for their accomplishments. While your partner or children may not realize the challenge of matching every sock, other women do.

2. The online Action Jam Sprint room is open sixteen hours each day with ten minutes between sprints. During these ten-minute breaks, a sense of community has developed as women share and become friends, and those working on like goals share tips.

3. Time and time again women commented on how much fun they were having. (Yes, fun and cleaning in the same sentence.) What was once a source of drudgery had become an anticipated time for community and accomplishment.

Shortly thereafter, I received a new coffeemaker, complete with morning brew functionality, but I have opted to maintain my "work-while-it-brews" routine. Each morning in this eight- to ten-minute period I unload the dishwasher, carry down and start a load of laundry, and fold the dry laundry (which I transfer before going to sleep at night). I wipe down the kitchen counters and peek in the fridge to make sure no one has absconded with ingredients needed for the night's dinner. I complete a quick walk-through of high-traffic areas to fetch miscellaneous items—the tape someone borrowed and did not return, the empty glass, a stray wrapper, pair of shoes, etc.

Realizing how much more managed my life felt with this ten-minute routine, I decided to implement a ten-minute evening sprint. At first, my goal was to do this right before bed. It did not take me long to realize that was not an effective solution for me. Just before bed I was too tired or plain old disinterested in cleaning. I moved this second sprint to right after dinner. I am up already clearing or washing plates, so I added a bit more time to tidy up the home before relaxing for the evening.

WHY THE SPRINT-SYSTEM WORKS:

- Sprinting creates a habit of spending realistic and regular cleaning time on home maintenance. While our "first pass" at a home that has not been tended to regularly will require more time, once the home is in order, sprinting allows easy maintenance for areas that could otherwise quickly get out of control.
- Sprinting follows one of success's golden rules: break things down. While a full day or afternoon of cleaning may seem daunting, we can handle many things for short increments of time.
- Sprinting helps us feel better because we are actively taking control of the home.
- Sprinting is realistic. Everyone can find ten to twenty minutes somewhere in the day!

TAKE A STEP FORWARD

Begin your own sprint routine. Aim for twenty minutes each day, either in one solid block, or two separate ten-minute increments. Write down the chosen time in your calendar. Find or purchase a timer within the next couple of days to maximize the sprint or join us online for moderated sprints.

REALITY CHECK

When we come across a new idea or begin a new program we may be reenergized and set high expectations. With sprinting, and any other change you desire to make routine and long-lasting, set the maximum goal to five days per week. Life interrupts and this gives it room to do so. If we do find additional time, wonderful — we exceed the goal. If we set a goal of seven days a week, 365 days each year, there is no room to overexceed, only room to underperform.

TOOLS, RESOURCES, AND REFERENCES

☑ Transform cleaning from fret to fun with a bimonthly free Saturday marathon sprint. Visit the website to view upcoming sprint times.

☑ A timer can be a revolutionary tool for life management. For tips and ideas on how to use a timer in other areas of your life follow the online link to the Timer Tips article.

☑ Take advantage of our moderated Housework Helpers Action Jam area providing a supportive, moderated sprinting environment seven days a week.

housework helpers
step 3

MERGE AND PURGE
The Six-Box System

"There are no menial jobs, only menial attitudes."—William John Bennett

Any areas marked as a "Merge and Purge" on your Housework Helpers Worksheet require a different solution than standard cleaning. Tackling a merge-and-purge area requires preparation to avoid common cleaning pitfalls. When women begin to clean such an area they often report:

1. A long-forgotten item is uncovered (photographs, letter, book) and attention is turned from merging and purging to a stroll down memory lane.
2. An uncovered item belongs in a different area of the home. For example, the Trivial Pursuit game is found in between baking sheets in the kitchen. The game is returned to the game area, where a vase from the dining room is discovered. The vase is returned to the dining room, only to find the bandages typically housed in the medical cabinet are on the dining room table. The process continues, one hundred laps of the house are completed, yet little overall progress is made.

When I set out to complete a "big home clean" (the type where you don't just move clutter from area to area but actually solve the clutter challenge), I used the system I had learned from many books in my home library. *Handle each item only once and sort everything into one of four categories: Store, Sell, Give Away, or Throw Away.* However, I found I had items that didn't fit into these categories, and I ended up doing the one hundred laps around the home. I customized the system by adding two more boxes—Put Away and Stow Away. These unique additions solved the challenge of working through my home and its clutter efficiently.

SUPPLIES
- Six large plastic containers or boxes
- Lined paper
- Tape
- Pen

> *I personally use four plastic storage totes plus two cardboard boxes. I chose the largest size I can fill and still carry without throwing out my back. The plastic storage bins and two cardboard boxes are the "ideal" solution, but if you do not have them on hand, or are not inclined to go out and purchase them, use any container you have. It is best to read through all of the instructions in this Step and then decide what type of container would best serve your purpose.*

Label the containers as follows:

Cardboard Box #1:	THROW AWAY
Cardboard Box #2:	GIVE AWAY
Plastic Container #1:	STOW AWAY
Plastic Container #2:	PUT AWAY
Plastic Container #3:	STORE AWAY
Plastic Container #4:	SELL

BOX CONTENT GUIDELINES

THROW AWAY

I won't offer much explanation on this one. The more you can put into this box, the simpler your life will become. As we all know, stuff uses energy. The less stuff you have, the less energy you expend taking care of it (dusting it, washing it, fixing it, etc.) and the more space you create for stress-free living. I use a box because a lot of my throw-away is paper, which I recycle. If you have a "mixed lot" of throw-away items, a garbage bag may be a better choice.

GIVE AWAY

Tape a piece of lined paper to the box. Anything you give to a charity or church should be tucked here.* When placing an item into this box, write the item name on the paper. When you take the box to the donation point, present the paper itemizing the box contents for validation. The organization can sign the paper as an itemized receipt of the contents for a charitable tax deduction. Some organizations will give you a different receipt. Staple the receipt and inventory list together for tax time.

*If you will be giving items to a friend or relative, create a box or bag with their name on it. You do not need to inventory the contents unless you so desire.

PUT AWAY

Undoubtedly, as we move through our homes we will find many things that are in the wrong place. Perhaps we were too busy and never gave a new item its "proper home," or perhaps Junior has a habit of bringing every toy into the kitchen and now you have plastic army men in your muffin-tin cups. Whatever the item, place it in the PUT AWAY box. If your home has a lot of stuff in the wrong place, consider making a couple of PUT AWAY boxes; for example, one for upstairs and one for downstairs.

STORE AWAY
If you find seasonal or infrequently used items taking up valuable space, reclaim space by carefully storing items in boxes and then storing the boxes in a garage, basement, or other storage area. Seasonal clothes and table wear only used on special occasions or during the holidays are a few examples. Make sure to label each box thoroughly so when the time comes, you can quickly find what you need. For my storage boxes, I use a sheet of lined paper and create an inventory. I then attach this in a plastic sleeve to the box. I label all four sides clearly with big letters to note the contents; for example, "summer clothes" or "Christmas lights."

SELL
Anything you choose to sell goes inside this box. However, there is a special rule for this box.

The Selling Rule

If you will be selling the items at a garage sale, the garage sale must occur within six months. Do not hoard items for years while waiting for the perfect garage-sale day. Trust me — there isn't one.

After moving from Milwaukee to Portland and back again, I was amazed to find I had amassed ten boxes of inexpensive trinkets for a garage sale. Six years had passed since I intended to have my garage sale, and my back seriously regretted the decision to crate these boxes back and forth across the country. The better choice would have been to donate them.

There are other ways of selling besides garage sales. In Portland we had a great clothing consignment store. You could take in up to thirty items per month. Each month as you brought in new items, a check was issued for any previous month sales. Check the Yellow Pages for consignment shops in your neighborhood.

If you have a digital camera, a bank account, and an email address, consider selling items on eBay (or any of the many consumer selling sites available). It only takes an hour or two to learn how to use eBay and it is a great way to sell items valued at $12 or more. (You can sell

---

> *lower price items, but I have found that with the listing fee and time involved, $12 is the lowest I like to go. Try it yourself and set your own "low limit.") If you do not have a digital camera, consider taking pictures with a regular camera and then have a disk supplied when your photographs are developed.*

STOW AWAY

The stow away box is for the items that give you a headache when trying to decide which box to put them in. Instead of huffing, puffing, and blowing up in frustration, put them in the STOW AWAY box. Make sure to tape a piece of paper to this box and write down what you stow. Include the date you create the box as well.

> ### The Stowing Rule
>
> *Once every six months, revisit each stowed box. Often when we look at these items fresh, we can easily decide whether to give them away, sell them, junk them, store them, or restow them. Thin your STOW AWAY boxes regularly.*

OTHER SYSTEM GUIDELINES

Begin in the room of your choice. Finish one room completely before starting another. Do not wander off to put an item away in another room; instead, place it in the "put away" box.

When a garbage bag or box is full, immediately take it your garbage area.

Do not let the boxes sit out for days on end. Put each box away within twenty-four hours.

Any boxes marked for donation should be taken to the donation point within thirty days.

TAKE A STEP FORWARD

Choose a room (or an area of a room) to begin with. For ideas, see any tasks you marked with Merge and Purge on the Housework Helpers Worksheet. Assemble your needed supplies, set a timer for twenty minutes, and dive in. Consider transferring all the Merge and Purge tasks from your Housework Helpers Worksheet into their own list. Set a goal to work through one of these areas every few days, each week, or monthly. The regimen frequency will depend on your schedule and how large the merge and purge area.

TOOLS, RESOURCES, AND REFERENCES
☑ If you are facing serious clutter, consider our Extreme Home Makeover Workshop: Ten Weeks to the House You Want.

housework helpers
step 4

Create Your Master Task List

"If a man is called to be a street sweeper, he should sweep streets even as Michelangelo painted, or Beethoven composed music, or Shakespeare composed poetry. He should sweep streets so well that all the hosts of heaven and earth will pause to say, 'Here lived a great street sweeper who did his job well.'"—*Martin Luther King, Jr.*

Transforming the Housework Helpers Worksheet into a Master Task List provides a systematic, low-stress guide to household maintenance. Make a photocopy of the Master Task List or find the copy in the Companion Workbook. Have this handy to refer to while reading through the instructions.

Transfer each item from your Housework Helpers Worksheet onto the Master Task List. As you list each item, mark the specific day the task will be done. For example, if loading and unloading the dishwasher is on your list to do daily, place a checkmark in all seven boxes to indicate it will be done each day of the week. If sweeping the kitchen is on your list for two times per week, place two checkmarks to indicate which days sweeping will be done.

Continue transferring items until all items that are done at least weekly are on this list. For now, leave any tasks that are done monthly, or less than monthly, on the Master Maintenance Worksheet.

When finished, you have created a Master Task List to maintain your home, broken down by daily routine. Before deeming this list complete, it is important to do a success evaluation.

Every Two Weeks   Every 3 Weeks

Weekly Master Task List for _____

Task	Mon.	Tue.	Wed.	Thu.	Fri.	Sat.	Sun.

LOWERING EXPECTATIONS
Find five tasks and decrease the frequency of how often they are done. Women tend to always aim for perfection, so finding five should be relatively easy. Are there any other tasks that could be done less frequently? Are there any tasks that could be eliminated altogether?

IS THERE ANYTHING ON YOUR LIST THAT SOMEONE ELSE CAN DO?
Do you have kids who should/could be doing chores? (Chore and reward systems are covered in the Family Matters Mini-Makeover.) Could your partner help with some of the items on your list? Before you decide children or a partner will not help and everything is up to you—ASK! Place a star next to any tasks you could delegate to remind yourself to delegate instead of do. Create a weekly routine checklist of delegated tasks and post where family members can easily see what they need to do.

IS YOUR PLAN REALISTIC?
Do tasks need to be completed as often as scheduled? While we do not want homes that are disasters, we want to avoid obsessing and overworking if a task is not a family priority. Every task on this list takes away from time you could otherwise spend with self, family, friends, or community. Does this schedule allow time for your life priorities?

SIMPLIFY WHERE POSSIBLE
Some tasks are easier the more often they are done. If you leave shower cleaner in the tub and spray after each shower, you will not end up with a "clean shower/tub task" that takes two hours. If you do not periodically maintain the shower, then it will be labor-intensive and difficult.

Yearly Master Task List

Task	Jan.	Feb.	Mar	Apr.	May	Jun.	Jul.	Aug	Sep.	Oct.	Nov	Dec.

WORKING WITH MONTHLY TASKS

The tasks left on the Master Maintenance Worksheet are those done monthly or less than monthly. Make a photocopy of the Yearly Planning Task List or find the copy in the Companion Workbook. This task list works much like the weekly list, except columns are divided into months of the year instead of days of the week.

Use the same steps to transfer remaining tasks to the yearly list. Place a checkmark to indicate in which month or months the task will be completed.

USING THE SYSTEM

- As each new month starts, consult the Yearly Task List for any of your infrequent tasks that are due to be done that month. Add them to one of your weekly lists.
- Do not be intimidated by your tasks! If you find you are avoiding a specific task, either break it down into easier steps, join an online sprint for motivation and accountability, or make it the first task tackled on a given day and get it over with. If you repeatedly avoid a task, this is a red light that: (1) the task is not a priority, (2) you need help with this task, and (3) you need to break the task down into smaller steps.

When life happens and you find yourself off schedule by a day, or a week, or a month, do not abandon the system. Pick up with the current day of the week. Do not worry about what was missed; focus on what needs to be done this day.

If you are motivated by crossing off completed to-do items, print copies of your routine lists by day; for example, Monday Task List, Tuesday Task List. Keep the list in your CAN and check off items as you complete them.

TAKE A STEP FORWARD

Transfer each item from your Master Maintenance Worksheet onto either the Master Task List or the Yearly Task List. Keep your lists in your Headquarters behind the Planning tab.

TOOLS, RESOURCES, AND REFERENCES

- ☑ Additional copies of the Master Task List are available on the website.
- ☒ View samples of completed Master Task Lists or download templates in Adobe PDF, Microsoft Word, or Microsoft Excel format.

housework helpers
step 5

Mastering Meal Planning

"Life itself is the proper binge." —*Julia Child*

According to a recent study, come 4:00 p.m., 70 percent of people have no clue what they are having for dinner. Eight percent of families only have dinner together once a week. Looking at those statistics, it is no wonder that fast-food and unhealthy convenience foods are a billion-dollar industry and we are facing unprecedented weight gain in our children. In addition to the nutritional decline, we face a "connection" decline. Our great-grandparents had meals together two to three times *per day* while we are lucky to have one meal together two to three times *per week*. The family meal acts as a "mini family meeting" where we come together and share our days and our lives. When this is lost, we begin to lose touch with one another.

These statistics encouraged me, a notorious noncook, to recreate the dinner hour in our home. This Step is designed to help you create a plan to enjoy a homemade family meal five days per week. Before we get started, let me cover the most common questions I hear when menu planning comes up.

WHAT IF WE ARE ALL RUNNING EVERY WHICH WAY DURING THE DINNER HOUR?
Set a dinner time by choosing when the most family members can be present, for example six o'clock. Stick to this time every day. Let everyone know dinner is at 6:00 p.m. and you expect family

members to work around the dinner hour when possible. If they don't, that's okay. Don't cancel the dinner hour because someone cannot attend.

THERE IS ONLY ME (OR MYSELF AND ONE OTHER PERSON). SHOULD I COOK A FULL MEAL EVERY NIGHT?

My husband travels three to five days per week and we rarely know his schedule more than twenty-four hours in advance. At first, I felt meal planning was impossible under these circumstances. I often had dinner planned or in the oven, and then he would be called to travel. More often than not I would feed my two-year-old and just make myself a snack instead of preparing a full dinner. But then I realized that my daughter deserved the sit-down dinner hour, even at age two. And I did, too.

THE QUICKEST WAY TO DESIGN A MEAL PLAN

Before diving into cookbooks and scouring online for recipes, take a survey among family members. Explain you are creating a series of weekly menu plans and by participating in the idea phase, family members can influence what is served. Ask each person for an idea (or two or three). If everyone moans when your husband says liver and onions, ask for a different meal idea. The goal is to find meals that work for everyone or the majority. Do not forget to add a few of your own choices!

Once you have the meal list it is time to pick the meals for the plan. Before choosing, consider the following:

DO YOU USUALLY EAT OUT IN A GIVEN WEEK?

If so, you may want to plan for five or six days instead of a full seven. I always do my plans based on five home-cooked meals. I like doing it this way because I don't end up with spoiled food or leftovers that are not used.

CONSIDER USING THE SAME MAIN INGREDIENT TO MINIMIZE COSTS AND SPOILAGE.

For example, you might want to feature beef one week and chicken another to take advantage of store sales. If the weekly flyer shows beef is on sale, choose a beef week.

Important Tip

Do not include recipes you "want to try" but have not yet been approved by the family. A Master Meal Plan requires a bit of thinking when it comes to the shopping list, so you don't want to have to rework it. If you end up with a recipe that no one will eat again, then you have to remove these ingredients from the list. I use my weekly meal plans during the week, and experiment with new recipes on the weekends.

Once you have selected five recipes, place them in page protectors (to protect from spills and splats while cooking). I use letter-sized page protectors you can find at any office store and keep them in a three-ring binder (one of the binders on your supply list is for this purpose). Most of my recipes are printed off the computer or cut from magazines. I tape any recipe cut-outs to a regular piece of paper and then place inside a protector. If you use recipe cards, purchase photo album pages which come in a variety of sizes and easily fit recipe cards. Even if you can cook the recipe from memory, create a recipe page and place it in a page protector. In the event you are unavailable, someone else could easily step in and do the cooking.

CREATING THE MASTER SHOPPING LIST

I generate my master shopping lists by pencil, and then transfer them to the computer so I can print multiple copies. Begin by looking at a recipe and writing down the ingredients by group: produce, canned goods, pantry/spice, meat, dairy. Move on to the next recipe and add its ingredients to your list. If it uses the same ingredient as one of the previous recipes, increase the amount already on your list. For example, if you have a recipe that calls for two onions and then come across a recipe that needs another onion, change your "two onions" to "three onions." (You can see why pencil works well the first time around.)

Once you have finished listing all the ingredients, you are almost done. Check to make sure you have enough side dishes to serve with your main entrees. If you don't, repeat the process of finding a few recipes for sides, and add those ingredients, plus any bread and salad fixings to your shopping list.

Photocopy this list or type into your computer and print multiple copies. Place the shopping list with the supporting recipes. This menu is now ready to serve your family well for years to come! Simply take the shopping list, check it against what you have on hand, purchase any items you need, and follow the recipes for a week of wonderful dinner hours.

TAKE A STEP FORWARD

Over the next fourteen days, schedule the following steps on your calendar:

- Talk to your family to generate recipe ideas.
- Locate, write or type out recipes and place in page protectors.
- Write down all ingredients.
- Create a master shopping list for the weekly menu.

More Meal Planning Ideas

Our online Meal Planning Club offers a new menu each week and step-by-step instructions and ideas for creating customized meal plans. You will find menus themed for holidays, cooking with a slow cooker, bulk cooking, make-ahead meals, and much more. To learn more, check out our Mastering Menus section online.

TOOLS, RESOURCES, AND REFERENCES

- ☒ Visit the Rush Hour Cook area of www.brooknoelstudio.com for complete weekly menus with shopping lists scaled to two, four, or six servings.

conclusion

The Challenge Continued...

"Life isn't about finding yourself. Life is about creating yourself." —*George Bernard Shaw*

T.S. Eliot said, "What we call the beginning is often the end. And to make an end is to make a beginning. The end is where we start from." Although you are near the end of this book, my hope is that your journey is only beginning. While a book must end, the needs to grow and discover do not. Even though you have worked through the Steps, each season of your life brings new experiences and perspectives. Each time you work through a Step, you will gain new insight for applying that Step to your life.

NEW BEGINNINGS

After you have worked through the book once, you can continue the voyage of self-discovery by completing a new Snapshot and Action plan each month. Take the life area in most need of attention from the Action Plan and locate it on the chart below. Work through the suggested Steps. If you finish, move onto the next area. Continue this practice monthly. Save your Snapshot and Action Plans as a record of your journey.

If you would like to continue growing and adding new Steps and Mini-Makeovers, visit www.brooknoelstudio.com

The Toolbox	Time Management	Information Management	Relationship with Significant Other	Relationship with Children	Relationship with Friends/Family	Money Management	Self-Time	Attitude and Outlook	Self-Esteem	Household Maintenance	Health	Energy	Religion and Spirituality	Community	Meal Planing
Step 1: Meet the Catch-All Notebook	✓	✓													
Step 2: The Three Step Action List	✓		✓	✓	✓								✓		
Step 3: How Do You Start Your Day?			✓	✓			✓	✓	✓		✓	✓	✓		
Step 4: The Catch-It Envelope	✓	✓								✓					
Step 5: Moments of Magic			✓	✓	✓			✓	✓		✓	✓	✓		
Step 6: Soul Food							✓	✓	✓				✓		
Step 7: The Five-Minute Rule	✓	✓								✓					
Step 8: The Five-Minute Relationship Miracle			✓	✓	✓			✓					✓		
Step 9: The Five-Minute Motivator	✓	✓								✓	✓	✓			
Step 10: Self-Sabotage and Self-Belief							✓	✓	✓		✓	✓			
Step 11: Avoiding Burnout and Over commitment	✓							✓			✓	✓			
Step 12: Your Personal Power Hour	✓	✓													✓
Step 13: Have an Ugly Day	✓	✓				✓				✓					✓
Step 14: Giving Up the Cape	✓	✓	✓	✓	✓	✓	✓	✓	✓	✓	✓	✓	✓	✓	✓
Step 15: Nightly Reflection	✓	✓					✓	✓		✓		✓	✓		
Mini-Makeover: Chaos and Clutter Clearing															
Step 1: Chaotic Confessions	✓	✓						✓		✓			✓		
Step 2: The True Cost of Clutter	✓	✓				✓		✓		✓			✓		
Step 3: Unraveling the Complicated Life	✓	✓						✓	✓	✓	✓	✓			
Step 4: Create a Space								✓		✓			✓		
Step 5: Junk Mail, Anyone?		✓								✓					

The table column group heading: Snapshot and Action Plan Life Areas

Snapshot and Action Plan Life Areas

	Time Management	Information Management	Relationship with Significant Other	Relationship with Children	Relationship with Friends/Family	Money Management	Self-Time	Attitude and Outlook	Self-Esteem	Household Maintenance	Health	Energy	Religion and Spirituality	Community	Meal Planning
Mini-Makeover: Self, Sanity, and Centeredness															
Step 1: Is Your Glass Half-Full or Half-Empty?			✓	✓	✓			✓	✓				✓	✓	
Step 2: Defining Decisions	✓		✓	✓	✓	✓		✓	✓				✓	✓	
Step 3: Reconciling Your Emotional Energy Account							✓	✓	✓		✓	✓	✓	✓	
Step 4: Operation Handbag	✓									✓					
Step 5: Girls' Night Out					✓		✓	✓	✓		✓	✓		✓	
Mini-Makeover: Money Matters															
Step 1: Determining Your Value Number						✓									
Step 2: Why We Buy						✓									
Step 3: Create a Spending Station						✓									
Step 4: Managing Day-to-Day Spending						✓									
Step 5: The Impulse Spending Solution						✓									
Mini-Makeover: Family Matters															
Step 1: Operating the Errand Express	✓	✓				✓				✓		✓			
Step 2: Do Unto Others…			✓	✓	✓			✓	✓				✓	✓	
Step 3: Host a Happy Half Hour			✓	✓				✓	✓				✓		
Step 4: Who is that Person across the Table?				✓				✓	✓						
Step 5: Chore and Reward Systems that Work	✓									✓					
Mini-Makeover: You've Gotta Have Friends															
Step 1: Organizing the People in Your Life	✓		?		✓			✓	✓				✓		
Step 2: The People Principle	✓				✓			✓	✓				?		
Step 3: Make a List, Checking it Twice	✓				✓			✓	✓				?		
Step 4: Connecting					✓			✓	✓				?		
Step 5: Here's Looking at You			✓	✓	✓		✓	✓	✓		✓	✓	?		

Snapshot and Action Plan Life Areas	Time Management	Information Management	Relationship with Significant Other	Relationship with Children	Relationship with Friends/Family	Money Management	Self-Time	Attitude and Outlook	Self-Esteem	Household Maintenance	Health	Energy	Religion and Spirituality	Community	Meal Planning
Mini-Makeover: Joy and Purpose-Filled Living															
Step 1: Values Our Lens to View the World	✓		✓	✓	✓			✓	✓		✓	✓	✓	✓	
Step 2: Giving Back								✓					✓	✓	
Step 3: Where Are You Going?			✓	✓	✓		✓	✓	✓				✓	✓	
Step 4: Create a Vision Statement	✓		✓	✓	✓			✓	✓		✓	✓	✓	✓	
Step 5: The Art of the Invisible Blessing			✓	✓	✓			✓					✓	✓	
Mini-Makeover: The Worn-Out Woman															
Step 1: Ask for Help	✓							✓	✓	✓	✓	✓			
Step 2: The Invisible Coach							✓	✓	✓		✓	✓			
Step 3: Self-Coaching Strategies							✓	✓	✓		✓	✓			
Step 4: Fighting Back Fatigue								✓			✓	✓			
Step 5: Creating Personal Power Scripts	✓						✓	✓	✓		✓	✓			
Mini-Makeover: Here's to Your Health!															
Step 1: The Simplest Diet in the World								✓	?		✓	✓			
Step 2: That Meal in the Morning								✓	?		✓	✓			
Step 3: S.O.S. for Stress								✓	?		✓	✓			
Step 4: Let's Get Moving!								✓	?		✓	✓			
Step 5: Wading into Water								✓	?		✓	✓			
Mini-Makeover: Housework Helpers															
Step 1: Master Maintenance Schedule	✓									✓		✓			
Step 2: Sprint Your Way to Success	✓							✓	✓	✓		✓			
Step 3: Merge and Purge: The Six-Box System		✓								✓					
Step 4: Create Your Master Task List	✓	✓								✓					
Step 5: Mastering Meal Planning	✓									✓					

appendix 1

Worksheet Quick Reference Guide

Additional Resources for the Journey: Your Quick-Reference Guide.

PRINTABLE WORKSHEETS

Use the quick-reference index on page 344 to easily locate worksheets throughout the book. All of these worksheets can also be printed full-sized from www.brooknoelstudio.com

Location	Worksheet	Page
Getting Started Step 2	The Snapshot	20
Getting Started Step 3	Action Plan	29
Toolbox Step 10	Self-Friendship Table	95
Toolbox Step 15	Power Hour Worksheet	115
Toolbox Step 15	Short-Term Worksheet	116
Toolbox Step 15	Active Task List Worksheet	117
Toolbox Step 15	Financial Record Worksheet	118
Money Matters Step 3	Wants Ledger	196
Money Matters Step 3	Bills Ledger	197
Money Matters Step 3	Actual Spending Ledger	198
Family Matters Step 1	Errands Checklist	210
You've Gotta Have Friends Step 1	Organizing Relationships Worksheet	232
You've Gotta Have Friends Step 4	Prioritizing Relationships	244
Housework Helpers Step 1	Housework Helpers Worksheet	328
Housework Helpers Step 4	Weekly Master Task List	344
Housework Helpers Step 4	Yearly Master Task List	346

appendix 2

Additional Resources

The following resources by Brook Noel may be of interest based on the life areas you are working on. You can learn more about any of these resources at www.brooknoelstudio.com

	Time Management	Information Management	Money Management	Self-Time	Attitude and Outlook	Self-Esteem	Household Maintenance	Health	Energy	Meal Planning
E-book/Workbook: Getting Things Done!	✓	✓								
Online Course: Simplify Your Life: Clearing Physical and Emotional Clutter	✓	✓					✓		?	
E-book/Workbook: The Procrastination Solution	✓	?		?	✓	?		?	?	
E-book/Workbook: The Paper Pile Solution	?	✓					✓			
E-book/Workbook: Financial Freedom		✓	✓		?					
E-book/Workbook: A Do-it-yourself Self-Discovery Workshop				✓	✓	✓		?	?	
E-book/Workbook: 10 Day Attitude Make over	?			✓	✓	✓		?	?	
E-book/Workbook: A Do-it-Yourself Self-Esteem Workshop	?	?		✓	✓	✓				?

acknowledgments

Writing acknowledgments to this book feels like trying to give an Oscar speech where it would be impossible to remember all the names that played a part in bringing this book to life and helping the second edition evolve. Let me say thank you first to all of you who have been with me in this program. Each day I thank God for your belief, growth, trust, and sharing.

I would like to thank my "Orlando Girls" from our first and second conventions for spending a weekend with me. I could not have found a greater reward than seeing and hearing your stories. Janet R., thank you for your faith and the great appreciation letter and special Challenge clips you made. I look at the letter often.

To the original "Yahoo Group"—please enjoy credit for much of what this book has become. When the first edition was released, I didn't know if I should create an e-group because I wasn't sure if anyone would post. Thank you for posting, sharing, helping to hone the vision, and providing the feedback to help me and the program grow.

I cannot say enough about the volunteers who have jumped in throughout the years to help this program reach more women. From those who assist in small roles to the group of phenomenal women who have been part of the online sprint moderating team, both past and present, thank you. A special thanks to those moderators celebrating a two-year anniversary: Lyn, Linda M., and Debbie S.; and to Linda M. for providing the Word of the Day.

Paige, Amy the Prosecutor (as Sammy says), Mary Ellen in NJ, Bonnie with the Laugh of the Century, Felicia, Ryland, and Debbie S., the "quote queen," thank you for the emails and communications throughout the years of development. Every time I see your names I smile.

These acknowledgments would not be complete without recognizing those outside of the incredible community of this program who have contributed equally to the reality of this vision.

Shana, I will have an Editor of the Year award delivered. Thank you for helping this book to become all it can be, and for letting this project unfold in the crazy way it did, supporting it all the while. To Dojna Shearer, Sabrina Baskey-East, and those behind the scenes I have not yet met doing layout and covers and all the zillion components it takes to make a book—I look forward to meeting you to thank you in person. To Michael Gulan, my onsite spare brain, thank you taking good care of me, my family, and my life while I dove into this project.

On the home front—Sammy Noel, you remain the #1 contributor and inspiration. Thank you for being patient and helping Mom by also embracing this vision and giving up some of your time to help me help others. Few people can do this as an adult, let alone at age twelve. For my husband, Andy, thank you for believing in me from age sixteen. There are many points in this journey when logic would have said to turn around; thank you for having the faith to defy logic and join me in pursuing dreams instead. To my mother who deserves the most credit for stating since childhood, "Brook— you can do anything you set your mind to," and teaching me obstacles were stepping stones I had to grow to reach.

And lastly, Lyn—may all your socks find matches.

about the author

Brook Noel is the author of nineteen books, specializing in life management and balance for today's busy woman. Noel is best known for going "beyond the book" by creating a whole experience to interact and support her readers. She delivers free motivational podcasts, online Q&A chats, message board interaction, in-person free "coffees" when she travels, and free newsletters delivered regularly to tens of thousands of readers. Her greatest passion is the Make Today Matter Life System Online which is the basis for *The Change Your Life Challenge.* "I feel like everything I have done or experienced in life has culminated in this program and book. The program isn't just about family time, or menu planning, or procrastination, or organizing—it is about every major area of a woman's life."

Noel was recognized in 2003 as one of the Top 40 Business People Under the Age of 40 by the *Business Journal.* She was a spokesperson for the Home Business Association and was featured in their top entrepreneur issue. She is an expert for Club Mom and a spokesperson for the Whirlpool Corporation specializing in the time crunch of busy moms.

Noel has conducted workshops for and/or appeared on/in: *CNN Headline News, ABC World News, FOX Friends, Woman's World,*

Our Children (National PTA Magazine), *Los Angeles Times*, Cedars-Sinai Medical Systems, *Parent's Journal*, *Booklist*, *Foreword*, *Independent Publisher*, University of Washington, UW-Milwaukee, University of Michigan, Single Parents Association, AM Northwest, *Town & Country*, *New York Post*, "Ask Heloise," Bloomberg Radio—and hundreds of other publication, shows, and stations.

Brook lives in Wisconsin with her husband, their thirteen-year-old daughter, a golden retriever, a black lab who thinks her name is "Kitty," a Puggle named Roxie, and one very large cat named Tom. She invites readers' feedback at

www.brooknoel.com